The Complete PowerShell Training for Beginners

Start from absolute zero, and learn to use the Windows PowerShell as it was meant to be used

By Abdelfattah BENAMMI

Dedication,

To my lovely students who enrolled in my Video training course and enjoyed it by leaving high number of positive reviews and who encouraged me to create this book version of the course

If you are not one of my video training students and want to give it a try, I am going to offer you a discount price to enroll into my course and enjoy it with 30-day money back guarantee

Visit this link to go directly to the course with active discount:

http://bit.ly/powershell19

TABLE OF CONTENTS

5

1. Before we Start

1.1.   What to expect from this book?

Welcome to the course! This training is suited for you either if you work with both Windows or Linux, it will allow you to perform maintenance tasks on local and remote systems (including network devices). We will cover not only the basics of the PowerShell language (variables, strings, hash-tables, operators, providers and drivers) but also give you advices on the best way to think on solving problems with a consistent strategy for programming. When more advanced you will be able to understand and code with the basic functionality of regular expressions.

To introduce myself a little bit, I'm a system and network administrator graduated on 2008 at the Institute of Applied Technology and started using this amazing programming language back in 2009, since then I've been learning and improving on this knowledge.

1.2.   Introduction to PowerShell

In order to access the Microsoft Windows Commandline we can go to "Start" -> "Execute" -> "CMD". We can see that it was the first implementation of a Commandline interface, since then they are improving so the commands can be better remembered. Almost all tasks that we do in the windows graphic interface can as well be done in the Commandline interface. Just to give an example we will create a shared folder on the graphical interface and show how it would be mapped as a drive letter on the Commandline interface. Let's go to "Windows Explorer" -> "C:" -> Create a New folder ->Right Click it -> On "Sharing Tab" click on "Share" button -> Choose "Everyone" -> "Add" -> "Share" Button. Now this folder is shared on the local network. It can be accessed locally on this URL: **\\127.0.0.1\New Folder**.

In order to create a folder mapping it to a drive letter on the command line we can use this command: **net use z: "\\127.0.0.1 New Folder"**. Bear in mind that the drive letter you chose must have been available. Now the shared folder is mapped as driver. We can see that we need to have that command and its syntax in mind before doing this operation, from this simple example we can start to see how the old CMD was not so intuitive (logical). The new Microsoft PowerShell try to overcome this difficulty creating commands that are both logical and easy to remember as we will see in the next sections.

2. Orientation and Requirements: Getting Ready for PowerShell

2.1. Discovering Windows PowerShell: Console Orientation

Even being an advanced PowerShell user, we advise you read this section because here we present some fundamental knowledge to build on. PowerShell comes on 2 different choices: Console and ISE. In our last example, we showed how to access the old Windows Command Line Interface (CMD), in order to access the new PowerShell, we need just to hit "Start" -> Type: "PowerShell" and the different options will be presented:

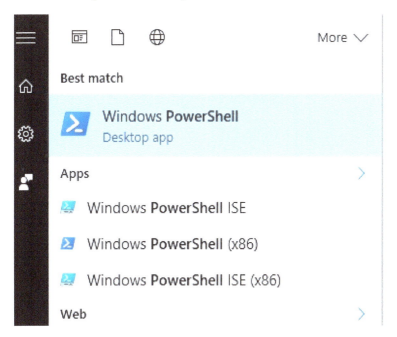

Figure 1: Example different PowerShell options available.

On this example, it appears the two different versions twice because the computer is for architecture x64, hence, allowing to choose from x86 versions for specific purposes. As we open the PowerShell we can see how different the native console interface is different from the CMD.

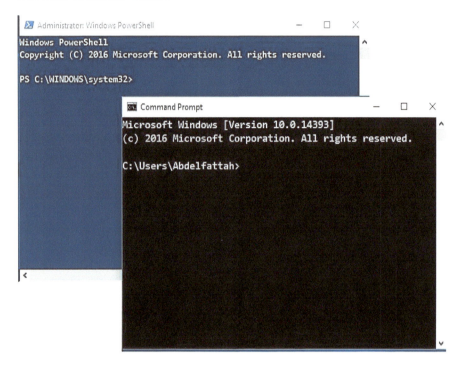

Figure 2: Side-by-side difference from PowerShell (left) and native CMD (right).

Note that on the PowerShell Commandline the prompt has a "PS" before the name of the folder we're at, this not happens on the CMD console. We can also star PowerShell inside the CMD Console, in order to this, simply type: PowerShell -> ENTER. We can see that the color of the console doesn't change but it shows the "PS" before the current folder just as if you would see on opening it directly from the graphical interface. One other way of accessing the PowerShell is double-clicking on its executable file. To discover the executable file, on the PowerShell options listed on Figure 1, right click it -> "Properties" -> "Open and Find Location". Knowing the path, you can reach it later directly navigating on the folders too. To open the PowerShell faster you can pin it to the taskbar or start menu, these are also options available when you "Right Click" on the PowerShell program.

One very important advice is **ALWAYS** open the PowerShell **as administrator**, it is necessary because most of commands (~80%) we will use on this course will only work if we are running as Administrator. When you right-click on the PowerShell this is the second option presented just below the "Open" option.

So far, we have covered only the first PowerShell option, we also have available the PowerShell ISE that will be better presented latter.

2.2.   PowerShell version table

The Microsoft PowerShell may come in different versions with its own restrictions; these are summarized on the table below:

Version	Desktop OS	Server OS	.NET required
2	Windows XP/Later	Windows Server 2003/Later	2.0 or 3.5
3	Windows 7/Later	Windows Server 2008/Later	4.0 Full
4	Windows 7/Later	Windows Server 2008/Later	4.0 Full

Table 1: Different versions of PowerShell with corresponding .NET framework requirements and compatibility for Desktop and Server Windows versions.

The PowerShell version walks together with the .Net Framework; basically, when we install/upgrade the .NET Framework it is common that the same package is responsible for installing/upgrading the PowerShell as well. To find out what

11

PowerShell version you have you can issue to a very simple command (remember to open PowerShell as Administrator): **$PSVersionTable.** On typing commands, you can always use the "TAB" button on your keyboard to let the console auto complete it for you, for instance, when issuing the aforementioned command, you could simply type: "$PSVersion" and then "TAB" key so it automatically auto complete for you.

```
Windows PowerShell

Windows PowerShell
Copyright (C) 2015 Microsoft Corporation. All rights reserved.

PS C:\Users\Abdelfattah> $PSVersionTable

Name                           Value
----                           -----
PSVersion                      5.0.10586.494
PSCompatibleVersions           {1.0, 2.0, 3.0, 4.0...}
BuildVersion                   10.0.10586.494
CLRVersion                     4.0.30319.42000
WSManStackVersion              3.0
PSRemotingProtocolVersion      2.3
SerializationVersion           1.1.0.1


PS C:\Users\Abdelfattah>
```

Figure 3: Example of the command showing the current PowerShell version

On Figure 3 we can see that the installed PowerShell version is the 5 (PSVersion).

2.3.   Customizing PowerShell for your Comfort

In the first time, you open the PowerShell you will notice it comes with standard font and background. Depending on the font used it may be harder to distinguish different characters like comma (,) from punctuation mark (.). To change the font used on the console we can do the following: *Right Click on the PowerShell title bar -> Properties -> Tab "Font"*. The default font is "Raster Fonts", a suggested font is "Consolas" either with boldface or not. You can also choose the size as well. I use the size 14.

On the "Layout" tab we can change the "Screen Buffer Size" that changes the size of the console inside the window. If you choose a buffer size bigger than the window it will appear a scrollbar. We recommend you always choose a Width buffer to be the same as the Window Width (otherwise, it would always appear a horizontal bar). Even if horizontal bars are not much for a concern for you, bear in mind that on some commands that show object lists it may present you with problems since the PowerShell always fills the screen from the right to the left (in these specific cases). It is important to note that this behavior was fixed on the version 5.

On the height, it is not a problem to have a Buffer height bigger than the screen height since we are usually used to "scroll down", however, if you choose a big "Windows Height" it may become a problem if that height is bigger than your screen size height (it would always appear to be "cropped" on the bottom). It is best to choose a window height that is lower than your screen height.

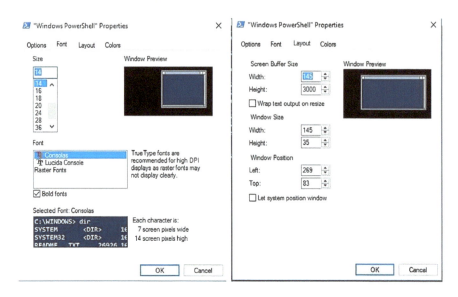

Figure 4: Configurations on Font and Layout PowerShell console

2.4.   Discovering PowerShell Integrated Script Environment (ISE)

Now we are going to cover the other PowerShell option called: PowerShell ISE. It is an integrated environment that allows us to quickly develop, test and search for documentation on the same window. Remember to always start your PowerShell **running as Administrator**. If you have previous experience on programming on the native batch file scripting, you know that the customary way of creating and testing a script only with default windows tools would be as follows:

- Create a file on some folder with "Right Click" -> New -> "Text Document"

- Rename that document to change its extension: "Right Click" -> Rename

- Change extension to .cmd

14

- Edit it with notepad: "Right Click" -> Edit

- Insert some code, for instance: calc.exe

- Save the document

- Close it

- Double-click the .cmd file

On this example, we just created a simple batch script that when executed opens the Calculator. To avoid this actions and provide the user with more productivity, Microsoft created the ISE environment so all these steps can be avoided. Let's take a look at the environment itself.

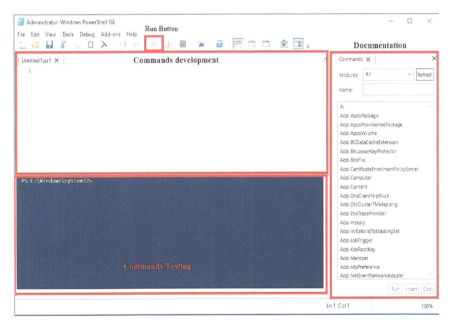

Figure 5: Overview of PowerShell ISE and 4 main parts.

At the PowerShell ISE we have 4 main parts, the first one is the "Commands Development" in which we can enter our code freely as if we were creating a script in Notepad on the previous example. For each line of code, you enter here, it will be automatically entered on the console below ("Commands Testing" part) with its corresponding output.

The "Documentation" part is very useful because commands are grouped in modules; therefore, you can also select a module and scroll down to discover all available commands. If you have additional modules installed the will be automatically listed here. If you know some part of the command, you can search it by name. When using a command out of this section, it generates graphical inputs for all specific command options for you, when you fill all the options accordingly, just click "Insert" and it is inserted on the "Commands Testing" part. We will cover more details on modules later on this course.

After you write some code you can promptly test it just hitting the "Run Button" in with it runs everything you just typed. In our previous example, we could replace all these steps to just these ones using the ISE:

- Type: "calc.exe" on the "Commands Development" part

- Click the "Run Button"

So we can see how the PowerShell ISE offers us with productivity gain combining very important functions in just one screen.

3. Finding and Discovering Commands

3.1.   Windows PowerShell Commands Formulation

All commands that we use on PowerShell are called "Cmdlet", it was created in a way that commands are consisted on two words involving a **verb** and a **noun**. Because of this design choice we can see how the CmdLets were built for being both easy to use and to remember. For instance, the command "**Get-Date**" obtains the complete date at the time it was issued, notice that it starts with "Get" which is the verb and ends with "Date" which is the noun.

3.2.   Pssnapin and Modules Commands

In PowerShell, there is 2 different ways for defining Cmdlets and functions. These are provided by: "**PsSnapin**" and "**Module**". The PsSnapins are a collection of commands that comes from a provider built on .NET, compiled and linked to DLL files. The PsSnapins form the base of PowerShell and although they are not used so extensively as the modules, they provide the base in which modules build on. The next kind of commands is the "**Module**", they combine a collection of commands that are created to be used directly to the user. When we saw the PowerShell ISE, the menu at the right shows exactly all the Modules available with their respective Cmdlets provided.

3.3.   Discovering the different Pssnapin Commands

It is important paying attention to the PowerShell profile; it allows us to save information about your session so you can use it latter. When we open a new console window, not that it starts blank that happens because (by default) the PowerShell profile stays on RAM memory and is lost as soon as the console window closes. In order to take a look at what is saved on the profile we can use the following command: **"Get-PsSnapin –Registered"**. Profiles in PowerShell work a lot like the registry in Windows, for example, when we install a game, play it and reach a certain level (let's say 5), then we decide to uninstall the game but keep the profile, when we decide to install it again, it will import the profile and remember we stopped at the level 5 so you can keep playing from there.

When we use the command *"Get-PsSnapin"* it will show only the "Microsoft.Powershell.Core" PsSnapin because this is the one loaded by default regardless you ask to load it explicitly or not. It may seem overwhelming, but you don't need to focus on this point in memorizing this command buy try to understand how the software was built to work. We can use another command called: *"Get-PsProvider | -format list -name PSSnapIn"* which will show all available providers with their respective snapins.

```
PS C:\Users\Abdelfattah> Get-PSProvider | Format-List Name,PSSnapIn


Name      : Registry
PSSnapIn  : Microsoft.PowerShell.Core

Name      : Alias
PSSnapIn  : Microsoft.PowerShell.Core

Name      : Environment
PSSnapIn  : Microsoft.PowerShell.Core

Name      : FileSystem
PSSnapIn  : Microsoft.PowerShell.Core

Name      : Function
PSSnapIn  : Microsoft.PowerShell.Core

Name      : Variable
PSSnapIn  : Microsoft.PowerShell.Core

Name      : Certificate
PSSnapIn  :

Name      : WSMan
PSSnapIn  :
```

Figure 6: Example of listing available providers and snapins.

The providers group the functions provided by a PSSnapin, in this case, it shows only the providers of the Core PsSnapin.

3.4. Discovering the different Modules Commands

To list the modules that are loaded on the session we can use the command "*Get-Module*".

```
PS C:\Windows\system32> Get-Module

ModuleType Version    Name                                ExportedComma
---------- -------    ----                                -------------
Manifest   3.1.0.0    Microsoft.PowerShell.Management      {Add-Computer
Manifest   3.1.0.0    Microsoft.PowerShell.Utility         {Add-Member,
Script     1.1        PSReadline                           {Get-PSReadli


PS C:\Windows\system32> _
```

Figure 7: Using the command "Get-Module" to list the session loaded modules.

Another way to see the modules is at the ISE interface at the right side when we showed that it allows us to search even for modules that are not loaded. Another option is to navigate inside the PowerShell folder structure and see the different folders that provide different modules, for instance, we can go to: "C:\Windows\system32\WindowsPowerShell\v1.0\Modules" and each folder inside this will represent a different module.

Finally, there is a specific option for the "Get-Module" command explained above that instructs the PowerShell to list all the available modules of the system: **"Get-Module – ListAvailable"**.

3.5.   Adds Modules to the Current Session: Import-Module

Inside a PowerShell session we can use the F7 button to show the command history. The settings for command history can be changed at: Right Click title bar -> Options Tab -> Command History. From the list, we can choose one command and hit ENTER to execute it again. Another way of accessing the command history is just press the buttons "up and down arrow", it will present on screen the ones used, and they can be changed back and forth.

To import a module on the current session we can use the command: "Import-Module". For instance: "**Import-Module TroubleshootingPack**". After importing it, when we run the command for showing the current loaded modules (Get-Module from Figure 7) it will show now three modules loaded. Now that our module is loaded we can use all commands it provide, however, how do we find out what are these new commands (Cmdlets)? We can use another very usefulCmdlet for this purpose: "Get-Command -Module TroubleshootingPack".

```
PS C:\Windows\system32> Get-Command -Module TroubleshootingPack

CommandType    Name                                      Version    Source
-----------    ----                                      -------    ------
Cmdlet         Get-TroubleshootingPack                   1.0.0.0    TroubleshootingPack
Cmdlet         Invoke-TroubleshootingPack                1.0.0.0    TroubleshootingPack


PS C:\Windows\system32>
```

Figure 8: Example of using the command "Get-Command" to list available commands provided from a specific module

Note that each line on the row "Name" will list the Cmdlet provided from that specific module, in this specific case the TroubleshootingPack provides only 2 Cmdlets. If you use the "Get-Command" without the "-Module" option, it will display all available commands for all modules loaded on your current session.

20

3.6. Find the right command to accomplish a task

To list all available modules, simply run: **Get-Module - ListAvailable**.

```
PS C:\Windows\system32> Get-Module -ListAvailable


    Directory: C:\Program Files\WindowsPowerShell\Modules


ModuleType Version    Name                              Export
---------- -------    ----                              ------
Binary     1.0.0.1    PackageManagement                 {Find-
Script     3.3.5      Pester                            {Descr
Script     1.0.0.1    PowerShellGet                     {Insta
Script     1.1        PSReadline                        {Get-P


    Directory: C:\Windows\system32\WindowsPowerShell\v1.0\Module


ModuleType Version    Name                              Export
---------- -------    ----                              ------
Manifest   1.0.0.0    AppBackgroundTask                 {Disab
Manifest   2.0.0.0    AppLocker                         {Get-A
Manifest   2.0.0.0    Appx                              {Add-A
Script     1.0.0.0    AssignedAccess                    {Clear
```

Figure 8: Example of command "Get-Module -ListAvailable" output

The list of modules is shown with information about version, name and available commands that it provides. In order to load a module, we can use another very useful command: Import-Module. With this command, it is necessary only to specify the module's name to be loaded, for example: **Import-Module -Name PSScheduledJob**. After a successful module load the above command should return no output. In order to confirm that it has been loaded we can use the same command from Figure 8 but without the "-ListAvailable" option, in this case, it will show only the loaded modules of your session.

```
PS C:\Windows\system32> Import-Module -Name PSScheduledJob
PS C:\Windows\system32> Get-Module

ModuleType Version    Name                                      ExportedCo
---------- -------    ----                                      ----------
Manifest   3.1.0.0    Microsoft.PowerShell.Management           {Add-Compu
Manifest   3.1.0.0    Microsoft.PowerShell.Utility              {Add-Membe
Script     1.1        PSReadline                                {Get-PSRea
Binary     1.1.0.0    PSScheduledJob                            {Add-JobTr
Manifest   1.0.0.0    TroubleshootingPack                       {Get-Troub
```

Figure 9: Example of command "Get-Module" output

As we can see our recently loaded module is shown on line 4. The column "ExportedCommands" it lists all commands that each module provide. Since this list crops that information we can get it using (again) the other very useful command for that purpose: **Get-Command -Module PSScheduledJob**.

```
PS C:\Windows\system32> Get-Command -Module PSScheduledJob

CommandType     Name                          Version     Source
-----------     ----                          -------     ------
Cmdlet          Add-JobTrigger                1.1.0.0     PSScheduledJob
Cmdlet          Disable-JobTrigger            1.1.0.0     PSScheduledJob
Cmdlet          Disable-ScheduledJob          1.1.0.0     PSScheduledJob
Cmdlet          Enable-JobTrigger             1.1.0.0     PSScheduledJob
Cmdlet          Enable-ScheduledJob           1.1.0.0     PSScheduledJob
Cmdlet          Get-JobTrigger                1.1.0.0     PSScheduledJob
Cmdlet          Get-ScheduledJob              1.1.0.0     PSScheduledJob
Cmdlet          Get-ScheduledJobOption        1.1.0.0     PSScheduledJob
Cmdlet          New-JobTrigger                1.1.0.0     PSScheduledJob
Cmdlet          New-ScheduledJobOption        1.1.0.0     PSScheduledJob
Cmdlet          Register-ScheduledJob         1.1.0.0     PSScheduledJob
Cmdlet          Remove-JobTrigger             1.1.0.0     PSScheduledJob
Cmdlet          Set-JobTrigger                1.1.0.0     PSScheduledJob
Cmdlet          Set-ScheduledJob              1.1.0.0     PSScheduledJob
Cmdlet          Set-ScheduledJobOption        1.1.0.0     PSScheduledJob
Cmdlet          Unregister-ScheduledJob       1.1.0.0     PSScheduledJob
```

Figure 10: Example of command "Get-Command -Module PsScheduledJob" output

The name column shows the name of all available commands for the module: PSScheduledJob. This command list is also useful to remember that, in PowerShell, it is common to have some built-in commands that are dash separated on the following format: VERB-NOUN. It is important to repeat that if you notice all above commands, the first word before the dash is always an action verb and the second is always a noun. This simple rule makes it easier for understating new commands.

With VERB-NOUN organization in mind, it can be remembered that the Get-command allows us to filter the command list specifying whether if we want only commands that are equal a specific VERB or NOUN. It even allows us to specify both at the same time and also using Wildcards. Our next example shows exactly that possibility: **Get-Command -Module PsScheduledJob -Verb set -Noun *scheduled***

```
PS C:\Windows\system32> Get-Command -Module PsScheduledJob -Verb set  -Noun *scheduled*

CommandType     Name                        Version     Source
-----------     ----                        -------     ------
Cmdlet          Set-ScheduledJob            1.1.0.0     PSScheduledJob
Cmdlet          Set-ScheduledJobOption      1.1.0.0     PSScheduledJob


PS C:\Windows\system32>
```

Figure 11: Example of "Get-Command" allowing specifying either verb and noun

As we can see, we could list all commands that have the verb "Set" and also the word "scheduled" in the middle of the respective noun.

This particular example also lets us to introduce the concept of wildcard. Wildcards allow for flexible specification on filtering texts. Every time we use the * wildcard it means "any character". If in our previous example the "-Noun" were "*task" it would list only the first two commands since it would process: "All commands with Noun that begins with any character (*) and ends with the word "task". In a similar way, if the "-Noun" was "cluster*" it would only list the first command since it would process: "All commands with the Noun that begins with "Cluster" and ends with any character (*). If we specify a wildcard with no respective results, it would show no commands, for instance, "-Noun *dir*". Finally, wildcards are very useful and used not only on PowerShell but on a variety of different systems as well (Google searches, other programming languages, etc.).

3.7. PowerShell Module Path Environment Variable

Depending on the PowerShell version some Cmdlets can have slight different names and/or syntax. Remember that to find out your version you just need to type "**$PSVersionTable**", all the examples we'll cover are considering the version 4.

To find out what folders PowerShell use to look for modules we can use another very useful variable called: "**$env:PSModulePath**".

Figure 12: Example of the variable "$env:PsModulePath"

Note that it shows 3 different folders separated with semicolon, the first path is specific to the current user session, in this way the user can copy a module to that folder and use it without needing to have administrator access. The second and third folders are system wide; therefore, when you copy a module to that folder (which will need administration privileges) it will be available for all users on that computer (the third one was showed earlier too). Some programs (when installed) can provide PowerShell modules as well (maybe as extra options for the user to interface in different ways with it).

When we use the Cmdlet "**Get-Module –ListAvailable**", before exhibiting all available modules it shows the folder in which these are; take a look again to Figure 8.

Some modules have what is called "auto-load feature". It means it is integrated tightly with PowerShell core system; the main benefit for the user is the module's ability to load itself automatically when some of its Cmdlets are used. That feature was introduced in PowerShell 3, from there on; all modules that come as default with the PowerShell have this feature. If you have the version 4, you can test this doing the following:

✓ On a new PowerShell session, issue the Cmdlet: "**Get-Module**"

✓ Now issue a Cmdlet from an unloaded module, for instance: "**New-AppLockerPollicy test**"

✓ Now run again the "**Get-Module**" Cmdlet.

You will notice that now the "Get-Module" Cmdlet shows also the AppLocker module as loaded. If you are using PowerShell version 2 or 3, you can load it manually too using the Cmdlet: "**Import-Module –Name AppLocker**".

3.8. Aliases: Linux Commands into PowerShell

Aliases allow us to use abbreviated and/or smaller names for commands that are otherwise bigger or harder to remember. Taking as example the "Photoshop Program", many people call it: "PS" which is an abbreviation easier to remember, type and speak.

Aliases in PowerShell accounts for the same benefits. It will be presented below 3 examples of the original Cmdlet and its default aliases built-in PowerShell to better illustrate this feature:

Cmdlet "**Get-ChildItem**" allows us to see the contents of a folder, since this is a rather big command; PowerShell has some aliases built-in for it: "**dir**" and "**ls**". The "**dir**" is for making it easier for users coming from the old CMD Console (on that console this is the command used for the same purpose). The "ls" is for making easier for users coming from the Linux Commandline interfaces (at Linux the "ls" command is used for the same purpose too). Another alias is the "**gci**" accounts for each upper case letter of the original command.

Cmdlet "**Clear-Host**" is used to clear the prompt screen; it also has two different aliases: "**cls**" and "**clear**", respectively, both are commands from the CMD Console and Linux.

Cmdlet "**Get-Location**" returns to the user the current folder path, this Cmdlet is very useful when we are working with FTP servers (that allows us to easily transfer files between computers) and want to know exactly the current folder we're in. The Linux compatible alias is "**pwd**" and another short version of this Cmdlet is: "**gl**".

3.9.   Outline of Finding and Discovering Commands

In this session, we covered the basic ways in which we can discover and use PowerShell Cmdlets. To revise a few findings, we learned that the Cmdlet: "**Get-Command**" returns with all available Cmdlets (that belongs to loaded modules of your session). We also learned that we can filter this Cmdlet so it returns only the commands that match our specification:

- "**Get-Command –Verb get**" returns only Cmdlets that has as verb the term "get";

26

- **"Get-Command –Verb get –Noun job"** combines the example above and adds another restriction: now it returns only Cmdlets that has as verb the term "Get" and as noun the term "job";

- **"Get-Command –Verb Get –Noun *job*"** adds more flexibility for the command above making use of wildcard on the Noun parameter. That wildcard allows it to return all Cmdlets that have the term "job" in the middle of it.

```
PS C:\Windows\system32> Get-Command -Verb Get -Noun *job*

CommandType        Name
-----------        ----
Function           Get-PrintJob
Function           Get-StorageJob
Cmdlet             Get-Job
Cmdlet             Get-JobTrigger
Cmdlet             Get-ScheduledJob
Cmdlet             Get-ScheduledJobOption


PS C:\Windows\system32>
```

Figure 13: Example of a more elaborated use of the Cmdlet "Get-Command".

4. Interpreting the Help from Windows PowerShell

4.1. Introduction to PowerShell Help

If up until this point some examples that were given didn't work for you, don't worry. This might happen in case of your PowerShell installation is different from the one used on the making of this course. It is important to understand that different installation versions can differ a little bit on some functionalities, for example, if you have an installation version previous than 3, it won't have the "module autoload" feature we described on the last section.

Even though you can always use the Internet to search for some assistance and help on the getting to know better examples and syntax, there will be times when this option won't be available (for instance, if you are working on a server without internet access). In this section, we will learn how to get help from the PowerShell default available tools itself.

4.2. Updating your Most Important Resource: Help

Some Cmdlets in PowerShell make extensive use of parameters in order to allow more flexibility. When we saw the example of simple commands such as "Get-Location" or "Clear-Host" you noticed we didn't specify any parameters, just the command itself. Some Cmdlets need, by default, that you provide them with a set of minimum parameters in order to use it. One Cmdlet we'll use as example to illustrate this is the "**Start-Job**". If you type only this Cmdlet on the prompt, you'll notice it will ask you for the minimal obligatory parameters.

To find out the available documentation on a specific Cmdlet we can use: "**Get-Help start-job**" (this Cmdlet also has an alias: help).

```
PS C:\Windows\system32> Help Start-Job

NAME
    Start-Job

SYNOPSIS
    Starts a Windows PowerShell background job.


SYNTAX
    Start-Job [-ScriptBlock] <ScriptBlock> [[-InitializationScript] <ScriptBlock>] [-ArgumentList
    <Object[]>] [-Authentication <AuthenticationMechanism> {Default | Basic | Negotiate |
    NegotiateWithImplicitCredential | Credssp | Digest | Kerberos}] [-Credential <PSCredential>]
    [-InputObject <PSObject>] [-Name <String>] [-PSVersion <Version>] [-RunAs32]
    [<CommonParameters>]

    Start-Job [-FilePath] <String> [[-InitializationScript] <ScriptBlock>] [-ArgumentList
    <Object[]>] [-Authentication <AuthenticationMechanism> {Default | Basic | Negotiate |
    NegotiateWithImplicitCredential | Credssp | Digest | Kerberos}] [-Credential <PSCredential>]
    [-InputObject <PSObject>] [-Name <String>] [-PSVersion <Version>] [-RunAs32]
    [<CommonParameters>]

DESCRIPTION
    The Start-Job cmdlet starts a Windows PowerShell background job on the local computer.

    A Windows PowerShell background job runs a command without interacting with the current
    session. When you start a background job, a job object returns immediately, even if the job
    takes an extended time to finish. You can continue to work in the session without interruption
    while the job runs.

    The job object contains useful information about the job, but it does not contain the job
    results. When the job finishes, use the Receive-Job cmdlet to get the results of the job. For
-- More --  ▪
```

Figure 14: Example of using the Cmdlet "Get-Help".

On figure 14, notice that it shows the Cmdlet syntax in two different ways of using it, along with it is also presented a simple description. Sometimes when the help is very complete it may be necessary to press the "spacebar button" to scroll it down. This Cmdlet allows it to filter and show only a subset of its information, imagine we want only it to show the examples related to a Cmdlet, just type: "**Get-Help start-job –Examples**". Depending on your

PowerShell version or update state it may show all the 6 examples for this Cmdlet or none. The idea here is to see all the different examples available and learn with them.

It is important to stress out that, in the specific case of the example provided, if you have a PowerShell version earlier than 3, you'll only manage to access this Cmdlet's help once you manually load the module it belongs to: AppLocker (as seen before, you can load it with: "**Import-Module –Name AppLocker**"). Also in such cases, you could use another option that will, automatically, open a browser and direct to the Microsoft online help (https://technet.microsoft.com) which has always the most up to date information: "**Get-Help start-job –Online**".

If the computer running the PowerShell prompt is not in a network with restricted Internet access, it is also possible to issue a Cmdlet that will bring all PowerShell internal help documentation to be updated: "**Update-Help**".

4.3.   Exploring the Help of any Command

As we saw earlier, you are now able to use the "Get-Help" Cmdlet in order to obtain more information about any unknown Cmdlet. From Figure 14 it is important to note that the documentation show 2 different ways of using the Cmdlet "Start-Job", let's go into some more details on how to read this information.

- **[-ScriptBlock] <scriptblock>**: This means that there is an obligatory parameter called "-ScriptBlock" and after you specify this parameter you'll need to specify also the value associated with it, this value must be of the type "scriptblock". Since only the parameter name (and not its value) is inside brackets, it means also that you can omit it and specify only its value directly, for instance: "Start-Job –ScriptBlock $test" and "Start-Job $test" would do the same thing. This is called "positioned parameter".

- **[[-InitializationScript] <scriptblock>]**: This means that there is a parameter called "-InitializationScript" and when using this parameter, you must provide its value after it of type "scriptblock". Since both parameter and its value are enclosed in brackets, you can't omit the parameter, so it can only be used explicitly.

4.4. Understanding Cmdlet Syntax and Symbols

Continuing from the previous examples and explanations, we saw that when a word on the help documentation starts with a dash (-) it means that word is a "parameter". Parameters allow the Cmdlet to receive more inputs for additional flexibility. We'll see the remaining options shown on Figure 14 and explain each one:

- **[-ArgumentList <Object[]>]**: Optional explicit (because both parameter and value type are enclosed in brackets) parameter called "ArgumentList" that accepts an array of values of the type "Object". Always when we encounter this construction "<type>[]" it means "an array of <type>". An array is a set of values together. In this particular case the type "Object" is a special case of variable that allows (on the same variable) different properties;

- **[-Authentication {Default | Basic | Negotiate | ...}]**: Optional explicit parameter called "Authentication" that accepts as value only the listed options enclosed in braces which are separated with vertical bars (pipes).

- **[-Name <string>]**: Optional explicit parameter called "Name" that accepts as value the type "string" (which is the type that defines a simple text or word);

- **[-RunAs32]**:Optional explicit parameter called "RunAs32" that has not associated value, hence, it is used only to make the Cmdlet aware that it's appearance means that this feature should be enabled/executed. These parameters that doesn`t use values are often referred as "flags".

It is important not confuse flags with obligatory parameters; if a parameter enclosed with brackets is not followed by a type enclosed in chevrons (angle brackets), it is an optional flag. Note that on Figure 14 there is a second line explaining another way of using the Cmdlet, experience shows that often the second line refers to the most common use of the Cmdlet. The syntaxes in lines 1 or 2 can`t be mixed otherwise the Cmdlet will not execute.

4.5.   Getting some real Syntax Examples of Commands

Now we are going to explain in a little more depth how the examples of the help documentation are provided.

```
PS C:\Windows\system32> help Start-job -Examples

NAME
    Start-Job

SYNOPSIS
    Starts a Windows PowerShell background job.

    Example 1: Start a background job

    PS C:\>Start-Job -ScriptBlock {Get-Process}
    Id   Name  State  HasMoreData Location   Command
    --   ----  -----  ----------- --------   -------
    1    Job1  Running True        localhost  get-process

    This command starts a background job that runs a Get-Process command. The command returns a
    job object that has information about the job. The command prompt returns immediately so that
    you can work in the session while the job runs in the background.
    Example 2: Start a job by using Invoke-Command
```

Figure 15: Example of partial output from command: "help Start-job -Examples"

32

Notice that on Figure 15 only the first (out of many more) example is illustrated. As can be seen the first Example explains how to use the Cmdlet in two different ways for doing the same thing. It also shows what appears (by default) on the prompt after the command is ran. In this particular case the "Get-process" Cmdlet is started as a Job; thus, it shows some control information about it (id, name, state, etc.). Finally, notice in this example (on the first command) that a value of type "scriptblock" can be specified enclosing code in braces.

In order to separate the command prompt where you`ll be testing the Cmdlets and the help information, you can choose to open the help documentation on a new window, for that you just need to use: **"help Start-Job -ShowWindow"**.

On the help documentation, each parameter is explained in detail showing information such as: whether is required or not, position, default value, it is accepted as pipeline input or accept wildcards.

4.6.   Positions, Required and Non-Required Parameters

Taking another Cmdlet as example to explain how it shown on the help documentation: **"help Get-EventLog -Full"**.

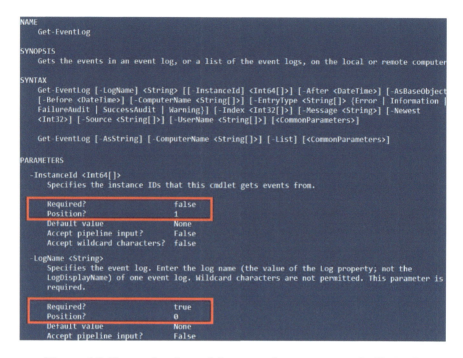

```
NAME
    Get-EventLog

SYNOPSIS
    Gets the events in an event log, or a list of the event logs, on the local or remote computer

SYNTAX
    Get-EventLog [-LogName] <String> [[-InstanceId] <Int64[]>] [-After <DateTime>] [-AsBaseObject
    [-Before <DateTime>] [-ComputerName <String[]>] [-EntryType <String[]> {Error | Information |
    FailureAudit | SuccessAudit | Warning}] [-Index <Int32[]>] [-Message <String>] [-Newest
    <Int32>] [-Source <String[]>] [-UserName <String[]>] [<CommonParameters>]

    Get-EventLog [-AsString] [-ComputerName <String[]>] [-List] [<CommonParameters>]

PARAMETERS
    -InstanceId <Int64[]>
        Specifies the instance IDs that this cmdlet gets events from.

        Required?                   false
        Position?                   1
        Default value               None
        Accept pipeline input?      False
        Accept wildcard characters? false

    -LogName <String>
        Specifies the event log. Enter the log name (the value of the Log property; not the
        LogDisplayName) of one event log. Wildcard characters are not permitted. This parameter is
        required.

        Required?                   true
        Position?                   0
        Default value               None
        Accept pipeline input?      False
```

Figure 16: Example of partial output from command: "help Get-EventLog -Full"

Note that the parameter "LogName" is mandatory and "InstanceId" is not. If we want to use this Cmdlet using the parameters in a positional way (omitting the explicit use of the parameter name), we need to know that "LogName" has the position 0 and "InstanceId", 1. If we use the parameters on the "named" way, it doesn't matter the position in which they appear:

- Get-EventLog "System" 16

- Get-EventLog -InstanceId 16 -LogName "System"

The two above commands do the same thing, the first passes parameter values on a "positional" way and the second on the "named" way.

4.7. Running the first Command with different parameters using the Help

In this section, we will show another example of using the help Cmdlet. Let`s get help on the Cmdlet "Save-Help". To accomplish this, we run: "**help Save-Help -Full**".

```
PS C:\Windows\system32> help Save-Help -Full

NAME
    Save-Help

SYNOPSIS
    Downloads and saves the newest help files to a file system directory.

SYNTAX
    Save-Help [-DestinationPath] <String[]> [[-Module] <PSModuleInfo[]>] [[-UICulture]
    <CultureInfo[]>] [-Credential <PSCredential>] [-Force] [-FullyQualifiedModule
    <ModuleSpecification[]>] [-UseDefaultCredentials] [<CommonParameters>]

    Save-Help [[-Module] <PSModuleInfo[]>] [[-UICulture] <CultureInfo[]>] [-Credential
    <PSCredential>] [-Force] [-FullyQualifiedModule <ModuleSpecification[]>] -LiteralPath
    <String[]> [-UseDefaultCredentials] [<CommonParameters>]


DESCRIPTION
    The Save-Help cmdlet downloads the newest help files for Windows PowerShell modules and saves
    them to a directory that you specify. This feature lets you update the help files on computers
    that do not have access to the Internet, and makes it easier to update the help files on
    multiple computers.
```

Figure 17: Example of partial output from command: "help Save-Help -Full"

Like before, we'll select some parameters and explain them below:

- **[-DestinationPath] <String[]>:** Mandatory parameter named "DestinationPath" that receives as value an array of string (list of text);

- **[[-Module] <PSModuleInfo[]]:** Optional parameter named "Module" that receives as value an array of module names;

- **[-Force]:** An optional flag called "Force";

35

As stated in its description on Figure 17, the Cmdlet "Save-help" is used to save help information on the filesystem. In order to test this Cmdlet lets create 2 folders: "C:\help1" and "C:\help2". We can use the first parameter to indicate that we want to save the help files in these two different folders that were just created. In addition, we can specify to the Cmdlet to save only three specific modules: "AppLocker", "BitsTransfer" and "ISE".

So, we can run the following:

- Save-Help -DestinationPath "C:\help1","C:\help2" -Module "AppLocker","BitsTransfer","ISE"

- Save-Help "C:\help1","C:\help2" -Module "AppLocker","BitsTransfer","ISE"

Notice that when specifying array values, we just need to separate them with commas (,). Both first and second commands do the same thing, the only different is: the first is the complete version that uses the "named" way for the mandatory "DestinationPath" parameter and the second omits it using the "positional" way.

After running the above commands, you can check your created folders to verify that files with extension .xml and .cab were created accordingly. You could change the values to, for example, include other folders, modules or even options (use other parameters such as: -force, UICulture, etc.).

4.8. Getting the Right Syntax by using the ISE

The Integrated Scripting Environment (ISE) at the documentation pane can be used to help on deciding which Cmdlet's parameters to fill and see the options on a more intuitive way. That pane is located on the right side of the screen (refer to Figure 5).

At the "Modules" select "All" and at "Name" you can type the Cmdlet name you want help with, in this case, "Save-help". After you select it, it's shown on the tab "Path" (the options are the same presented on the commandLine help documentation).

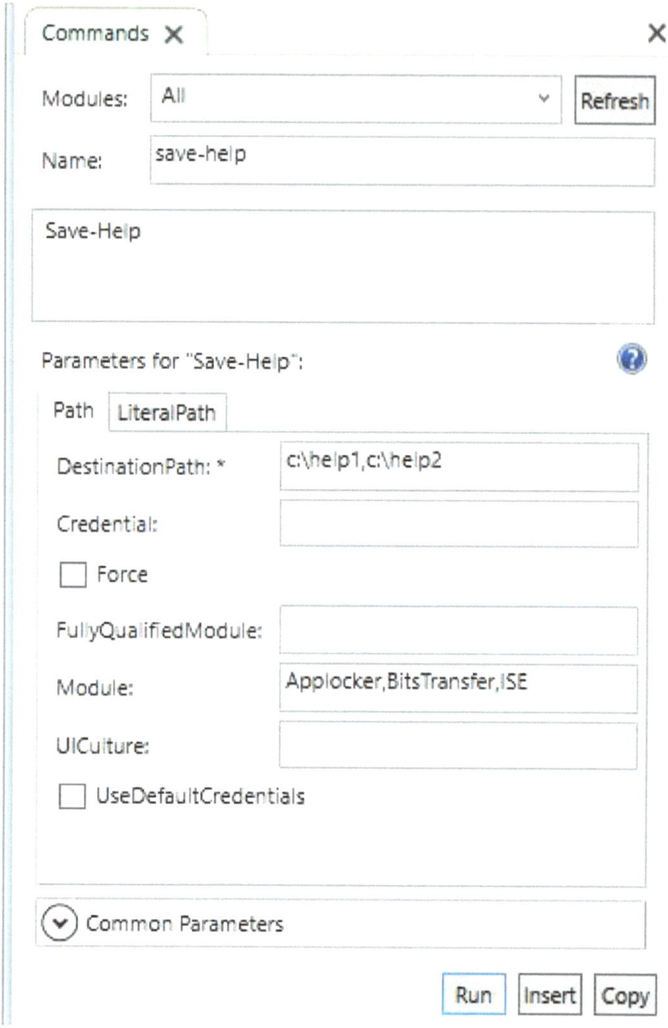

Figure 18: Example of the ISE use for inserting Cmdlet parameter's values.

After inserting the information on the right parameters there are three buttons available, respectively: "Run", "Insert" and "Copy". The first runs it directly at the command prompt, the second just copies it to the command prompt at the left side but without executing and the third copies it to the clipboard. The output generated will be the same we showed on the last section.

5. Running PowerShell Commands

5.1.　Introduction to PowerShell Commands: Applied Section

Until now we have seen how to find out what Cmdlets are available at the "Finding and Discovering Commands", after that we learned how to understand them when reading the help documentation ("Interpreting the Help") and now we are going to take a practical approach in allowing you to run the Cmdlets.

5.2.　Finding and Running the Command of Getting Process

Let's imagine we want to use a Cmdlet that will return a list of all the running Operating System's processes, something similar to what the "Task Manager" shows us but inside the PowerShell. To accomplish this, we need first to discover the name of that Cmdlet. At PowerShell ISE (remember to open as Administrator), let's try to discover all Cmdlets that have the term "process" in them (as the noun part): "**Get-Command –Noun '*process*'**", with this we'll be able to list all available Cmdlets that have as the noun a term that contains "process". This returns the following options:

- Debug-Process

- Get-Process

- Start-Process

- Stop-Process

- Wait-Process

Logically one can infer that the Cmdlet which accomplishes what we need is the "**Get-Process**" since the "Get" part implies that this Cmdlet is used mainly for showing purposes and the "process" implies that it shows OS (Operating System) processes. Running this Cmdlet, it will present similar results as you'd get at the "Task Manager". Since this Cmdlet has no required parameters, it'll always run successfully even without providing parameters. In order to know what parameters are available, we can always use the "Get-Help" Cmdlet: "**Get-Help get-process -Full**".

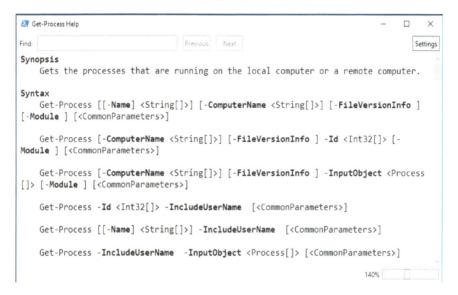

Figure 19: Result of "Get-Help Get-Process –ShowWindow" Cmdlet.

As can be seen there is no required parameters because all of them are enclosed with their respective values (when applicable) in brackets. The parameter "Name" accepts an array of strings (list of words separated with comma), so the "ComputerName". If we wanted to list all running processes that have the name "Chrome" we can issue: "**Get-Process – Name 'Chrome'**". Alternatively, we could use the ISE Cmdlet wizard to fill the attributes using the GUI (as shown at section 4.8).

40

```
PS C:\Windows\system32> Get-Process -Name chrome

Handles  NPM(K)    PM(K)     WS(K) VM(M)    CPU(s)      Id  SI ProcessName
-------  ------    -----     ----- -----    ------      --  -- -----------
    215      46   130012    108824   888    10,08      936   2 chrome
    269      20    33080     29364   747     2,42     1588   2 chrome
    215      19    29628     24604   734     1,39     3180   2 chrome
    109       8     1460      6664    85     0,02     3368   2 chrome
    317      22    41476     24104   292    10,28     3884   2 chrome
    306      44   124656     34924   896    16,94     5124   2 chrome
    401      45   107012     40884  1028    16,38     5448   2 chrome
    305      38    93700     81756   846     3,88     7000   2 chrome
    178       8     1352      5464    81     0,00     7528   2 chrome
    264      34    82232     43296   815     2,97     7696   2 chrome
   1597      52    69696     77996   455    57,03     7704   2 chrome
    214      19    28060     25440   728     3,22     7840   2 chrome
```

Figure 20: Output example of running "Get-Process –Name chrome".

5.3.   Understanding the String, Int32 and using a shortcut

From the last Figure, the list returned 12 entries, if it is required to be more specific, we can refer back to the Figure 19 and see other options available. We can use the parameter "Id" which allows the Cmdlet to filter and list a process that has a specific Id, for example: "**Get-Process –Id 7000**". This will list only one process that has the ID 7000. Since this parameter accepts array values (note that at the end of Int32 you see a '[]'), so we can specify more than one ID, or instance: "**Get-Process –Id 7000,7528**".

Now it's time to introduce the concept of shortcuts, parameter shortcuts were created to allow using parameters without needing to write their full names. For example, at Figure 19 we can see that the only parameter that starts with the letter "N" is the "Name", so we can use it only with its initial letter: -N. In this way, the Cmdlet invocation: "**Get-Process –N 'Chrome'**" will behave the same way

41

as in the example with the full parameter use provided on the previous section.

If you try to use a shortcut "-I" for "-Id" you'll notice that it'll throw an error stating that this abbreviation is ambiguous since there are, at least, one other parameter name that start with "I" (InputObject).

It's recommended to use shortcuts with caution since when reading a Cmdlet that makes use of it, one cannot easily infer to which parameter name it is referring to.

5.4.   Customizing the Error Message

In the previous section, when you ran the Cmdlet trying the shortcut "-I" an error appeared stating that it was an ambiguous abbreviation. That error message in black and red as, respectively, background and foreground colors. That colors can be changed by modifying properties of a default environment variable called "$host".

The property **"$host.PrivateData.ErrorBackgroundColor"** allows changing the background color and **"$host.PrivateData.ErrorForegroundColor"**allows changing the foreground color. If we want to change the background color to yellow and foreground color to black, it would be done like this:

- $host.PrivateData.ErrorBackgroundColor = "yellow"

- $host.PrivateData.ErrorForegroundColor = "black"

```
PS C:\Windows\system32> Get-Process -i 1
Get-Process : Parameter cannot be processed because the parameter name 'i' is ambiguous. Possible
matches include: -Id -InputObject -IncludeUserName -InformationAction -InformationVariable.
At line:1 char:13
+ Get-Process -i 1
+
    + CategoryInfo          : InvalidArgument: (:) [Get-Process], ParameterBindingException
    + FullyQualifiedErrorId : AmbiguousParameter,Microsoft.PowerShell.Commands.GetProcessCommand

PS C:\Windows\system32> $host.PrivateData.ErrorBackgroundColor = "yellow"
PS C:\Windows\system32> Get-Process -i 1
Get-Process : Parameter cannot be processed because the parameter name 'i' is ambiguous. Possible
matches include: -Id -InputObject -IncludeUserName -InformationAction -InformationVariable.
At line:1 char:13
+ Get-Process -i 1
+
    + CategoryInfo          : InvalidArgument: (:) [Get-Process], ParameterBindingException
    + FullyQualifiedErrorId : AmbiguousParameter,Microsoft.PowerShell.Commands.GetProcessCommand

PS C:\Windows\system32> $host.PrivateData.ErrorForegroundColor = "black"
PS C:\Windows\system32> Get-Process -i 1
Get-Process : Parameter cannot be processed because the parameter name 'i' is ambiguous. Possible
matches include: -Id -InputObject -IncludeUserName -InformationAction -InformationVariable.
At line:1 char:13
+ Get-Process -i 1
+
    + CategoryInfo          : InvalidArgument: (:) [Get-Process], ParameterBindingException
    + FullyQualifiedErrorId : AmbiguousParameter,Microsoft.PowerShell.Commands.GetProcessCommand
```

Figure 21: Examples of error message in (1) default behavior, (2) changing only the background to yellow and (3) changing the foreground to black.

If we exit the prompt, all these definitions will be lost and the default behavior (yellow background and black foreground) is restored. We can change that behavior when using profiles.

43

5.5.　Working with the Multi Values

As we saw on Figure 19, the parameter "Name" accepts an array of string because it's value definition has **[]** after the type (in this case, string) information, which means that we can specify more than one process name to filter on the Cmdlet separating the names with comma. For example: "**Get-Process –Name svchost, chrome**", additionally, we can specify the names enclosing them on single or double quotation marks, it would produce the same effect.

5.6.　Finding and Running Commands About Aliases

We have already discussed about aliases, but since this is an important topic, we'll get into more detail here. You can know more about aliases simply by reading the help documentation typing: "**help about_Aliases**". If you would like an option of a more practical approach, you can run a Cmdlet that shows all aliases available with their correspondent original Cmdlets issuing: "**Get-Alias**".

```
PS C:\Windows\system32> Get-Alias

CommandType          Name
-----------          ----
Alias                % -> ForEach-Object
Alias                ? -> Where-Object
Alias                ac  -> Add-Content
Alias                asnp -> Add-PSSnapin
Alias                cat  -> Get-Content
Alias                cd  -> Set-Location
Alias                CFS  -> ConvertFrom-String
Alias                chdir -> Set-Location
Alias                clc  -> Clear-Content
Alias                clear -> Clear-Host
Alias                clhy -> Clear-History
Alias                cli  -> Clear-Item
Alias                clp  -> Clear-ItemProperty
Alias                cls  -> Clear-Host
```

Figure 22: Example of "Get-Alias" Cmdlet.

44

At this list, you can find all aliases previously addressed. New aliases can also be created using the Cmdlet "**New-Alias**", to find out how it works, as always, we'll resort to the help: "**help New-Alias**".

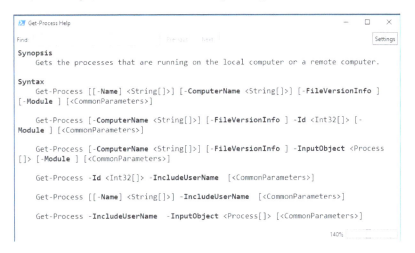

Figure 23: Documentation about the Cmdlet "New-Alias".

As can be seen from the previous figure, the "New-Alias" Cmdlet has two mandatory (and also positional) parameters: Name and Value where both are strings. If we want to create a new alias, we can use it in the following way: "**New-Alias –Name m –Value get-location**" or "**New-Alias m get-location**".

5.7.　　**Running some external Commands**

Besides the native PowerShell Cmdlets, we can also run external commands/programs at the PowerShell prompt. This behavior is similar to the old CMD console, as long as the executable files are inside any of the default folders contained in the environment path variable (**$env:path**), they will be available to be executed directly at the PowerShell prompt. Programs such as "ping", "Ipconfig", "nslookup", etc…. are available.

6. Working with Providers and Drives

6.1.   Introduction to Providers and Drives

At this chapter, we'll learn in more depth what providers are and how to use them. Don't forget to open your PowerShell prompt as Administrator.

6.2.   Understanding Providers and Drives

Providers components that make the data in a specialized data store available in PowerShell so that you can view and manage it. The data that a provider exposes appears in a drive and you access the data in a path like you would on a hard disk drive. To see the available providers, just run: "**Get-PSProvider**".

```
PS C:\Windows\system32> Get-PSProvider

Name              Capabilities                        Drives
----              ------------                        ------
Registry          ShouldProcess, Transactions         {HKLM, HKCU}
Alias             ShouldProcess                       {Alias}
Environment       ShouldProcess                       {Env}
FileSystem        Filter, ShouldProcess, Credentials  {C, E, F, D...}
Function          ShouldProcess                       {Function}
Variable          ShouldProcess                       {Variable}
```

Figure 24: Example of using the Cmdlet: Get-PSProvider.

Each different provider is listed at the "Name" column, its drives appear at the "Drives" column. The "Alias" provider has a drive called "Alias:" and by using that you can access all aliases as if you were interacting with a folder. The same behavior is for the remaining: "Env:", "C:", "D:", "Function:", "HKLM:", "HKCU:" and "Variable". The most commonly used providers are the "Environment", "FileSystem" and "Registry".

Specifically, for the "Registry" provider, the two drives have a direct relation on two specific registry upper-level folders:

- HKLM – **HK**ey_Local_**M**achine

- HKCU – **HK**ey_Current_**U**ser

If one wanted to browse the HKLM registry folder, one can simply execute: "**cd HKLM:**".

6.3. Working with Providers: Get-Itemproperty

On the previous section, we showed what providers are and how to use them explicitly. Providers are used throughout the PowerShell and its built-in Cmdlets, for this reason, we may interact with providers but in an indirect way, in other words, using Cmdlets that encapsulates the providers features as parameters.

To exemplify this usage, we can explain a new Cmdlet called: "**Get-ItemProperty**". This Cmdlet can extract all the property information from a given file and show it on-screen. The behavior of this Cmdlet is the same as accessing the properties at the user graphical interface (at "Windows Explorer" -> "Right click the File" -> "Properties").

As always, to find out how it works one can access it help documentation: "**help Get-ItemProperty**". At the help documentation it can be seen that this Cmdlet has only one mandatory parameter: "Path" that accepts an array of string (Get-ItemProperty [-Path] <string[]> ..). Supposing we create a file called "test.txt" at "C:\Help-ps", one example of usage is: "**Get-ItemProperty –Path C:\Help-ps\test.txt**".

```
PS C:\Windows\system32> Get-ItemProperty -Path C:\Help-ps\test.txt


    Directory: C:\Help-ps


Mode                LastWriteTime         Length Name
----                -------------         ------ ----
-a----        1/23/2017     21:11              0 test.txt


PS C:\Windows\system32> Get-ItemProperty -Path C:\Help-ps\test.txt | select *


PSPath            : Microsoft.PowerShell.Core\FileSystem::C:\Help-ps\test.txt
PSParentPath      : Microsoft.PowerShell.Core\FileSystem::C:\Help-ps
PSChildName       : test.txt
PSDrive           : C
PSProvider        : Microsoft.PowerShell.Core\FileSystem
Mode              : -a----
VersionInfo       : File:             C:\Help-ps\test.txt
                    InternalName:
                    OriginalFilename:
                    FileVersion:
                    FileDescription:
                    Product:
                    ProductVersion:
                    Debug:            False
                    Patched:          False
```

Figure 25: Example of using the Cmdlet: Get-ItemProperty (1) on the default behavior and (2) showing all attributes that are (by default) not explicit.

At the above figure, the first part shows the output of the Cmdlet given in the previous example. It can be noticed that this output is the same as the "ls c:\Help-ps\test*". This happens because the "Get-ItemProperty" has implicit (hidden) attributes that are not showed when the Cmdlet is exhibited in the default way. To show all existent attributes, it's needed to insert a pipe (|) after the Cmdlet and use another Cmdlet called "Select-Object" specifying it to select all attributes (*). In this way, all the attributes would be shown.

In order to discover more Cmdlets that interact with file's properties, we can discover doing the same we did before: "**Get-Command –Noun ItemProperty**". Notice that there's on Cmdlet called "**Set-ItemProperty**" that allows us to change a file's property.

48

6.4. Working with Providers: Set-Itemproperty

In order to know how the Cmdlet, Set-ItemProperty works, we need to check the help documentation: "**help set- ItemProperty-ShowWindow**".

```
Synopsis
    Creates or changes the value of a property of an item.

Syntax
    Set-ItemProperty [-Path] <String[]> [-Confirm ] [-Credential <PSCredential>] [-
Exclude <String[]>] [-Filter <String>] [-Force ] [-Include <String[]>] -InputObject
<PSObject> [-PassThru ] [-UseTransaction ] [-WhatIf ] [<CommonParameters>]

    Set-ItemProperty [-Confirm ] [-Credential <PSCredential>] [-Exclude <String[]>]
[-Filter <String>] [-Force ] [-Include <String[]>] -InputObject <PSObject> -
LiteralPath <String[]> [-PassThru ] [-UseTransaction ] [-WhatIf ]
[<CommonParameters>]

    Set-ItemProperty [-Name] <String> [-Value] <Object> [-Confirm ] [-Credential
<PSCredential>] [-Exclude <String[]>] [-Filter <String>] [-Force ] [-Include <String
[]>] -LiteralPath <String[]> [-PassThru ] [-UseTransaction ] [-WhatIf ]
[<CommonParameters>]

    Set-ItemProperty [-Path] <String[]> [-Name] <String> [-Value] <Object> [-
Confirm ] [-Credential <PSCredential>] [-Exclude <String[]>] [-Filter <String>] [-
Force ] [-Include <String[]>] [-PassThru ] [-UseTransaction ] [-WhatIf ]
[<CommonParameters>]
```

Figure 26: Help documentation of: Set-ItemProperty

As can be seen at the figure above, the Cmdlet has 3 mandatory parameters: Path, Name and Value. Respectively, the **Path** is to indicate over what file the operation will be executed, the **Name** refers to the name of the file's attribute we'll change and the **Value** is to set what information will be assigned at the **Name** attribute. As these parameters are mandatory, their order must be respected if using them in the implicit way.

In order to find out what attribute names are available, one can simply use the Cmdlet "Get-ItemProperty" using the pipe (|) and selecting all attributes (Select *) as was done at Figure 25. Since the Figure 25 is cropped at the end, so the full output of "Get-ItemProperty" is not shown. There is an attribute name called "isReadOnly" that controls whether the file is read-only or not. If we want to change that behavior and set the file to enable its read-only property, it's simply a matter of assigning the value "TRUE" to the attribute: "**Set-ItemProperty –Path C:\Help-ps\test.xt – Name isReadyOnly –Value $true**". After that you can check manually the file properties at the graphical interface and verify that it was changed (the Read-only checkbox is now "checked"). To disable the read-only attribute, one can simple change the **Value** to "**$false**". As happens with all Boolean types (types that accept as values TRUE or FALSE), they can interchangeably be assigned as the integers: 1 or 0, in this way, at the previous Cmdlet example, you can replace "$true" with "1" and "$false" with "0" at the **Value** parameter as well.

6.5.   **Working with Provider: Registry Provider**

The Windows registry allows flexible management of several different system's aspects. At this section, we'll give an example of PowerShell's ability to interact with the Windows registry and perform the same operations available at the graphical interface (using the regedit.exe program).

Let's assume we want to change the simple behavior or showing or not the known file types at the windows explorer. The easiest way to accomplish this is with the graphical interface: "Control Panel" -> "Appearance and Personalization" -> "Folder Options" -> Tab "View" -> "Hide extensions for known file types".

Another way of changing this behavior is interacting directly with the Windows Registry: Start "regedit.exe" -> Navigate to: HKEY_CURRENT_USER\Software\Microsoft\Windows\Current Version\Explorer\Advanced -> Double-click "HideFileExt". At that window, if the value is set to "1", the extensions will be hidden, if is set to "0", they won't be hidden.

At PowerShell (Always remember to open as Administrator), we can do the same thing by navigating to the "Advanced" key and change its property called "HideFileExt". It is important to say that at the PowerShell provider, each registry "key" (which stand as the notion of "folder" at the regedit.exe program) has its subkeys as properties of itself and not as files (as would happen at the regular file system). For this reason, if we navigate to the HKCU:\...\Explorer "folder" and list its contents, the children key's will be showed and with its corresponding subkeys as properties.

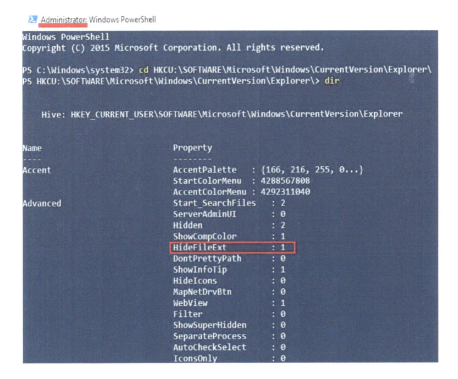

Figure 27: Example of navigating the registry and listing the "contents" of a key.

Notice that the key "Advanced" is shown as if it were a file and at the right side are its properties. Since we wanted to change the "HideFileExt" subkey, one can simply use the Cmdlet "Set-ItemProperty" we learned at the previous section:

- **Set-ItemProperty Advanced HideFileExt 1OR**

- **Set-ItemProperty –Path Advanced –Name HideFileExt –Value $true**

In the same way, we did previously, we could also use the Cmdlet Get-ItemProperty to find out the same information (all available attribute names).

Finally, the same result would be met if you provided the full registry path to the Cmdlet even not inside the registry provider "current folder":

- **Set-ItemProperty –Path "HKCU:\Software\Microsoft\Windows\CurrentVersion\Explorer\Advanced" –Name HideFileExt –Value 0**

7. Variables, Strings, HashTables and Core Operators

7.1.   Before starting this section

The previous sections were very important because they provided the very basic knowledge upon which we'll build on from now on. If you didn't understand any of what was taught earlier, please refer back to the text and try again. At this part, we'll learn how variables and PowerShell operators work.

7.2.   Introduction to Variables Strings

Remember to open the prompt as Administrator. PowerShell can handle not just variables but as well the very basic arithmetic operations. From the console we can just issue simple arithmetic operations, such as: "2+2", "10/5" or "(2*3)+(10/4)" and the PowerShell gives the answer right below.

Variables are special names that allow easy store of information and manipulation. At PowerShell, the variables all start with the dollar sign "$". For instance, "$a" is the variable "a" when used in PowerShell. We can assign values to variables using the equal sign "=". If we want to assign the number "3" to variable "a", we just need to do this: "$a = 3". To print a variable, we just type at the prompt and execute it. Once we assign a value to a variable, we can use it to make operations with numbers or other variables.

```
PS C:\Windows\system32> 5+5
10
PS C:\Windows\system32> $a = 5
PS C:\Windows\system32> $b = 3
PS C:\Windows\system32> $b
3
PS C:\Windows\system32> 5 + $b
8
PS C:\Windows\system32> $a + $b
8
PS C:\Windows\system32>
```

Figure 28: Example of arithmetic solving and variable assignment.

At Figure 28 we can notice examples of what was explained and also how the variable truly stores and represents the value it has been assigned to.

7.3. Different kinds of Variables

At the previous example, we used variable assignment for a particular type of value: Integer. PowerShell accepts different types of variables for holding different types of values, for instance: String (which is a group of characters), Float (numbers that have floating point), Boolean (type that stores either TRUE or FALSE), etc.

Depending on the way you assign values to variables, the PowerShell automatically finds out and convert that variable to that particular type. If you make like this: "**$c = '20'**", PowerShell recognizes that you enclosed the number in single (or double) quotes and converts the variable "$c" to the String type. Being a string, operations with this variable differ from those involving integers (which we saw earlier). If we add an integer with a String, PowerShell will just "Join" them and create a new string, so the result of "**$c + $a**" would be: "**205**". You can also assign $c as a

54

string without using the single/double quotes, you can explicitly state that at the variable assignment: **"$c = [string]20"**. In similar way, you can assign explicitly to integer as well: **"$c = [int]20"**, so the sum would now return: "25".

```
PS C:\Windows\system32> $c = "20"
PS C:\Windows\system32> $c + $a
205
PS C:\Windows\system32> $c = [int]20
PS C:\Windows\system32> $c + $a
25
PS C:\Windows\system32> $d = "Welcome"
PS C:\Windows\system32> $e = " to "
PS C:\Windows\system32> $f = "Morocco"
PS C:\Windows\system32> $d + $e + $f
Welcome to Morocco
PS C:\Windows\system32>
```

Figure 29: Example of string operations and assignments.

At the previous figure, we can see that the same behavior stands when assigning text strings and performing the "Add" operation, PowerShell simply joins them.

Another way of assigning String variables is hitting "ENTER" without closing the quotation mark in the same line, in this way, the PowerShell prompt will not compute the assignment but wait for more input, you can insert more text freely with line breaks and when you're done, you just can close it and hit "ENTER" twice to finish the assignment. This is very useful for when you need to insert memos or copyright information on variables (values that need line breaks).

7.4.   Discovering Windows PowerShell Arrays

Arrays are sets of information grouped on a single variable, they are very useful because they allow using less variables to archiving the same goal. Let's suppose we want to create a variable to hold integer values for the course numbers that a MCSE certification has. The array assignment can be done simply by separating the values with a "comma": "**$MCSE = 410,411,412,413,415**". When accessing the information, simply use the following notation: "$MCSE[0]" for 410, "$MCSE[1]" for 411 and so on. That number inside the brackets is called "array index". On arrays, the index always starts with zero (0).

```
PS C:\> $MCSE = 410,411,412,413,415
PS C:\> $MCSE[0]
410
PS C:\> $MCSE[4]
415
PS C:\> $MCSE
410
411
412
413
415
```

Figure 30: Example of array assignment and index operations.

Note that if you just type the array variable it shows all its contents. Arrays can have mixed value types as well, for instance: '**$mixed = 1,3,"world",$false,10**'

7.5. Discovering PowerShell Hash Tables (Associative Arrays)

In the previous example, we showed how to insert multiple values in a single variable, however, to way to recover these variables may not be appropriate for some cases where it would be desirable to access the values using names and not numbers. To solve this problem PowerShell has the Hash Tables, which allow associating arbitrary string names to corresponding variables.

In order to create a hash table, one simply need to do this: "**$ht = @{'en' = 'English'; 'fr' = 'French'; 'ar' = 'Arabic'}**". In order to access that information we can do in two different ways: "**$ht.en**" or "**$ht['en']**".

```
PS C:\> $ht = @{'en' = 'English'; 'fr' = 'French'; 'ar' = 'Arabic'}
PS C:\> $ht.en
English
PS C:\> $ht.fr
French
```

Figure 31: Example of creating and accessing hash tables.

More information about hash tables and arrays in general can be found using the help: "help arrays". We can always resort to the PowerShell help for learning more about the Cmdlets.

8. Regular Expression Basics

8.1.   Introduction to Regular Expression Basics

Regular expressions allow defining some special rules to match on strings in order to accomplish some objective. They are useful for extracting or replacing specific information on text that follows some specific pattern. This chapter is intended to give an overview of this subject and better introduce you to this concept.

8.2.   Understanding the Regular Expression Basics

To better explain the usage of Regex (Regular Expression) we'll work with a simple example. Let's suppose we want to verify whether a given IP address is in its correct format. To check this in PowerShell we can use the command "-match". As it's known, IP addresses are numbers that represent computer addresses as a block of 4 numbers separated with points (.) and these numbers can go from 0 to 255.

Some examples of IP addresses are: "127.0.0.1", "192.168.1.1", "200.200.200.200", etc. At Windows, we can access a remote computer specifying the IP address with two leading backslashes: "\\127.0.0.1". So, we'll use a Regex to validate such an address. The Regex command we'll explain is:

' "\\127.0.0.1" –match "\\\\\d{1,3}\.\d{1,3}\.\d{1,3}\.\d{1,3}" '

8.3.   Identify String Patterns: The Matches

Remember to open the PowerShell as Administrator. To know about Regex, we can try using the PowerShell native help: "**help about_Regular_Expressions**". At this documentation, we can find all information about this subject.

```
PS C:\> "Abdelfattah" -match "fat"
True
PS C:\> $Matches


Name                                            Value
----                                            -----
0                                               fat



PS C:\> "Abdelfattah" -match "FAT"
True
PS C:\> "Abdelfattah" -cmatch "FAT"
False
PS C:\> "ABDELFATTAH" -cmatch "FAT"
True
```

Figure 32: Examples of the difference between methods "-match" and "-cmatch".

To build on this concept, we'll learn some simple examples until we get to fully understand the command showed at the previous section. We can run ' **"Abdelfattah –match "fat"**' and it will return "True" because the term "fat" is contained at the "Abdelfattah" string. This method "**match**" has collateral effect of automatically changing the PowerShell internal variable called; "$Matches". This variable indicates what matches were processed as an array. If we want to check matches using case-sensitive verification, we need to use the "**cmatch**" method.

Now we'll introduce some Regex wildcards and special characters. Look at this example: ' **"123abc" –match "\d"** '. In this example the command returns "True" and when exhibiting the "$Matches" we can see that the matches were "1". This happens because the term "\d" matches a single digit (which is a number from 0 to 9). If we specify it twice, it will match the numbers 12, so if we specify it three times (\d\d\d), it will match "123". In order to avoid writing many "\d", we can use special control characters such as "+" which means "one or more" or "*" which stands for: "zero or more". See if we run: ' **"123abc" –match "\d+"** ' it will return: "123" since it matches all digits that are one after another.

In a similar way, there is also the special character: "\w" that matches any given text character, so if we run: ' **"123abc" –match "\w+"** ' it will match everything since it is all text.

```
PS C:\> "123abc" -match "\d\d"
True
PS C:\> $Matches

Name                                        Value
----                                        -----
0                                           12


PS C:\> "123abc" -match "\d+"
True
PS C:\> "123abc" -match "\w"
True
PS C:\> "123abc" -match "\w+"
True
```

Figure 33: Example of using "\d", "\w" and "+". The red underline represents what has been matched (you can always confirm checking the variable "$Matches".

You can change a little these examples using the combinations of special characters provided and learn more how the matches behave.

60

8.4.   Analyzing and Creating a Full Pattern

Now we have some knowledge to start understanding the full pattern provided at section 8.2. If we run: ' "\\127.0.0.1" –match "\d+" ' it will match only "127" because the rest of the number is separated with a dot (.), to recognize the dot and keep the pattern matching, we have to insert the dot at the pattern. To insert the dot, we need to escape it because in Regex the dot is a special character itself. To escape special characters in Regex we always use backslash. So, we can rewrite the command to: '"\\127.0.0.1" –match "\d\."', in this way it will match the dot. Since the IP address has 4 numbers separated with 3 dots, we can match the whole sting in this way:

- \d+\. – First number and the dot;

- \d+\. – Second number and the dot;

- \d+\. – Third number and the dot;

- \d+ – Fourth number (there is no '\.' because the IP address doesn't end with dot).

So, we can put it all together like this:

' "\\127.0.0.1" –match "\d+\.\d+\.\d+\.\d+"

In this way, it will match "127.0.0.1" successfully, however, it would match "1000000.222222222.365299944.224554788" as well since we used the "+" operator and it means "one or more". Since we know that IP addresses numbers go up to 255 (that contains three characters), we need to improve the Regex specifying that each digit (\d) can occur from 1 to 3 times only. We can specify this repetition restriction using braces "{}". So, we can replace the "+" with: "{1,3}":

' "\\127.0.0.1" –match "\d{1,3}\.\d{1,3}\.\d{1,3}\.\d{1,3}" '

```
PS C:\> "\\127.0.0.1" -match "\d+"
True
PS C:\> "\\127.0.0.1" -match "\d\."
True
PS C:\> "\\127.0.0.1" -match "\d+\.\d+\.\d+\.\d+"
True
PS C:\> "1000000.222222222.365299944.224554788" -match "\d+\.\d+\.\d+\.\d+"
True
PS C:\> "\\127.0.0.1" -match "\d{1,3}\.\d{1,3}\.\d{1,3}\.\d{1,3}"
True
PS C:\> "1000000.222222222.365299944.224554788" -match "\d{1,3}\.\d{1,3}\.\d{1,3}\.\d{1,3}"
False
```

Figure 34: Example refining the match pattern of the previous problem.

Until now we have created most of the pattern shown at section 8.2. Now we need to insert pattern code to include the two backslashes at the beginning of the original string. As the backslash is a special Regex character, it must be escaped as well, in order to do this, we just insert another backslash before it, so, to escape: "\\" we must use "\\\\", so the full Regex is formed:

' "\\127.0.0.1" –match "\\\\\d{1,3}\.\d{1,3}\.\d{1,3}\.\d{1,3}" '

8.5.   Example of Using this Regular Expression (Pattern Expression)

Now we are going to show a real example on using the Regex pattern matches. We can issue the command "ipconfig" that lists information about IP address information of our machine. The output of this command returns a line like this:

IPv4 Address . . . . : 192.168.137.1

In order to test this, we can copy this string and test it on PowerShell using the previous pattern example:

"IPv4 Address . . . . : 192.168.137.1" –match "\d+\.\d+\.\d+\.\d+"

This will return "TRUE" since the IP address will be recognized.

8.6. Making your Patter Expression Confidential

If, for example, we would like to hide our pattern or keep it inside a variable, we can simply make a simple assignment: ' **$ip = "\d+\.\d+\.\d+\.\d+"** '. We can use that pattern later just referencing it through the variable "$ip", so a command like this: ' **"IPv4 Address . . . . : 192.168.137.1" –match$ip**' will work and give the same behavior as the previous one.

```
PS C:\> $ip = "\d+\.\d+\.\d+\.\d+"
PS C:\> "Ipv4 Adress ..............................: 192.168.137.1" -match $ip
True
PS C:\> "my name is fettah" -replace "fettah", "Abdelfattah"
my name is Abdelfattah
```

Figure 35: Example of storing pattern information in a variable and using it.

It is important to stress out again the importance of keep learning PowerShell by yourself with lots of practice. Another user full example is using the method "replace" to replace some part of the text inside a string: '

"my name is fettah" –replace "fettah", "Abdelfattah" ', this will output the "fettah" as "Abdelfattah" because of the replacement.

9. Transaction: Manage transacted operations

9.1. Introduction to PowerShell Transaction

Remember to open the PowerShell as administrator. Run the previous Cmdlet to show all available providers "Get-PSProvider". At column "Capabilities" you'll notice some different names, basically, all providers have the "ShoudProcess" capability which means all of them implement a way of allowing built-in confirmation before executing actions. The "Filter" capability allow the use of wildcards for accessing the filesystem, the "Credentials" capability allows using different credentials when using the specific provider. Finally, the "Transactions" capability is applicable only to the "Registry" Provider and adds an extra layer to the Registry operations interface, it allows specifying a set of changes to be done and either applying them all (if successfully) together or failing them all together. As an analogy to a file edition, we can edit a file and when we press "close", only two things can happen: it is saved or it is not.

```
PS C:\Windows\System32> Get-PSProvider

Name            Capabilities                        Drives
----            ------------                        ------
Registry        ShouldProcess, Transactions         {HKLM, HKCU}
Alias           ShouldProcess                       {Alias}
Environment     ShouldProcess                       {Env}
FileSystem      Filter, ShouldProcess, Credentials  {C, E, F, D...}
Function        ShouldProcess                       {Function}
Variable        ShouldProcess                       {Variable}
Certificate     ShouldProcess                       {Cert}
WSMan           Credentials                         {WSMan}
```

Figure 36: Transactions Capability for the "Registry" Provider

9.2.   Discover the Cmdlets of the Transaction

As ways, we can firstly find out which CmdLets are available for using with transactions. For that purpose, we can issue: **"Get-Command   –CommandTypeCmdLet – ParameterNameusetransaction"**. This Cmdlet will list all Cmdlets that has any parameter that accepts the use of transactions. You can learn even more about transactions with "help **about_transaction"**. To find out all Cmdlets those have the term "Transaction" on its name: **"Get-Command –Noun Transaction"**.

Figure 37: List of Cmdlets that have "Transaction" on its name.

The Cmdlet names are self-explaining. It is important to note that a transaction has to be explicitly created (Start-Transaction), it can be recovered for further manipulation (Get-Transaction), it can be issued for execution (Complete-Transaction) and it can be restored (Undo-Transaction). The "Use-Transaction" is the option that CmdLets implement to allow their actions to be controlled by transactions.

9.3.   Start a New Transaction

The CmdLet to start a transaction is: "Start-Transaction". After executing this Cmdlet, the transaction is started and after that we can start manipulating the registry, for instance, create a new key called "foo" in HKCU: **"cd HKCU:"** and after that **"New-Item foo"**. Inside that key, we can create a sub key: **"New-ItemProperty –Path foo –Name Hello –PropertyType string –Value 'Hello World'"**.

```
PS C:\Windows\System32> cd HKCU:
PS HKCU:\> New-Item foo


    Hive: HKEY_CURRENT_USER


Name                        Property
----                        --------
foo



PS HKCU:\> New-ItemProperty -Path foo -Name Hello -PropertyType string -Value 'Hello World'



Hello        : Hello World
PSPath       : Microsoft.PowerShell.Core\Registry::HKEY_CURRENT_USER\foo
PSParentPath : Microsoft.PowerShell.Core\Registry::HKEY_CURRENT_USER
PSChildName  : foo
PSDrive      : HKCU
PSProvider   : Microsoft.PowerShell.Core\Registry
```

Figure 38: Creating a new Key "foo" in HKCU.

After executing these previous steps, you'll notice that the registry is changed after each Cmdlet execution, however, if we wanted them to be evaluated at once and have the ability to undo them easily, we can resort to the **"-UseTransaction"** (or its alias **"usetx"**) parameter. Please, erase the "foo" key before continuing.

Now, run all previous commands with the "UseTransaction" parameter:

- **New-Item foo –Usetx**

- **New-ItemProperty –Path foo -Name Hello – PropertyType string –Value "Hello world" –usetx**

At this time, you'll notice that the changes are not done yet (if checking with Regedit) because they have not been executed. We can use the CmdLets to show Registry information with the "-UseTransaction" flag, in this way, it will show the changes since we are taking the transaction into account: **"Get-Item foo –UseTx | Get-ItemProperty –UseTx"**.

To save the changes effectively, one need just to issue the Cmdlet: **"Complete-Transaction"**. Now you can go back to regedit and verify that all changes were, in fact, committed.

9.4. Get Information About the Active Transaction

The Cmdlet **"Get-Transaction"** allows checking information about the current transaction status. Before continuing, erase the key created at the previous example, after that, run the commands again using the transaction and, after that, run: **"Undo-Transaction"**. Now issue: **"Get-Transaction"**.

```
PS HKCU:\> Undo-Transaction
PS HKCU:\> Get-Transaction


RollbackPreference SubscriberCount      Status
------------------ ----------------     ------
             Error                0 RolledBack
```

Figure 39: Transaction status using "Get-Transaction".

The "**SubscriberCount**"lists how many transactions are active, in this case (after the undo-transaction) there are none. The "**Status**" indicates that all transaction actions were rolled back.

Now let's start 2 transactions using: "**Start-Transaction**" twice and ask the PowerShell to list with "**Get-Transaction**":

```
PS HKCU:\> Start-Transaction

Suggestion [1,Transactions]: Once a transaction is started, only commands
-UseTransaction flag become part of that transaction.
PS HKCU:\> Start-Transaction

Suggestion [1,Transactions]: Once a transaction is started, only commands
-UseTransaction flag become part of that transaction.
PS HKCU:\> Get-Transaction


RollbackPreference SubscriberCount Status
------------------ ---------------- ------
             Error                2 Active
```

Figure 40: Example of two active transactions.

If you run again "Undo-Transaction", all two transactions will be closed and not just the last one. If you run any command that uses transaction and that command results in error, again, all transactions will be cancelled. So, at the previous example if you run "**Get-Item 98989898 –UseTransaction**", it will cancel all two transactions as well.

9.5.   Rollback Preference of the Transaction

Until this point we learned how to create transactions and use them. As already known, when a command from a single transaction fails, all active transactions are closed automatically. At some scenarios, it makes totally sense since the transactions command may have some sort of dependence of each other. At other scenarios, we may want the PowerShell to just ignore the failed commands and keep all active transactions.

To accomplish this, when creating the transaction, an option can be used: "**Start-Transaction –RollbackPreference Never**".

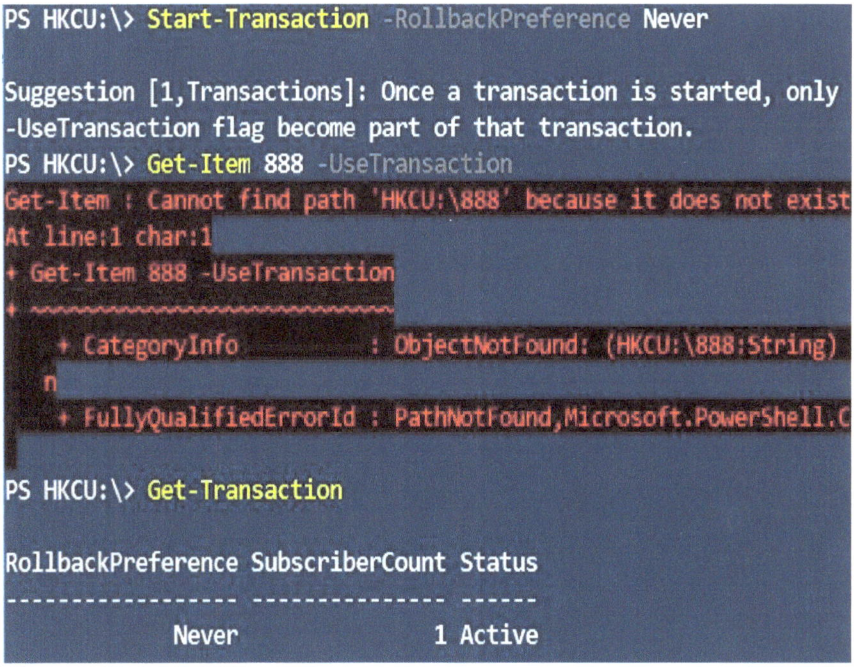

Figure 41: Example transaction with RollBackPreference and its behavior.

69

Note that after the failed command the transaction is still active. You can learn more from this option "**RollBackTransaction**" accessing the help ("**help Start-Transaction**").

```
-RollbackPreference <RollbackSeverity>
    Specifies the conditions under which a transaction is automatically rolled back. The default value
is "Error".

    Valid values are:

    -- Error:  The transaction is rolled back automatically if a terminating or non-terminating error
occurs. "Error" is the default.
    -- Terminating error: The transaction is rolled back automatically if a terminating error occurs.
    -- Never: The transaction is never rolled back automatically.

    Required?                    false
    Position?                    named
    Default value                Error
    Accept pipeline input?       false
    Accept wildcard characters?  false
```

Figure 42: Example of help documentation on "RollbackPreference"

The default option is "Error", because of that we saw the behavior of closing the transactions at previous examples. If you create a transaction as seen on the examples before, you'll notice that the transaction only rollback or commits when active action is taken at the user side. Transactions can be created with rollback timeouts as well, in this way, at the transaction creation a timeout can be specified and if you don't complete it before the time runs out, it is automatically rolled back.

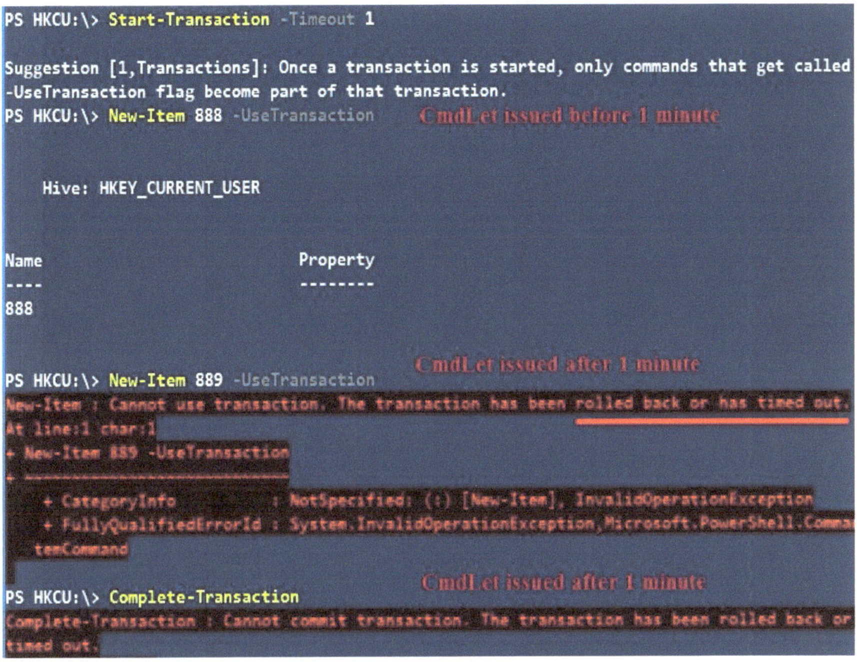

Figure 43: Example transaction timeout.

Note from Figure 43 that when the "**New-Item**" Cmdlet is called using the transaction before the timeout, it runs fine, however, the subsequent one fails and even the "**Complete-Transaction**" as well because the time ran out and it has rolled back automatically.

9.6.   Commit the Transaction

To commit the transaction, we need simply to run: "**Complete-Transaction**". It is important to know that when there is more than one active transaction, the commands issued with "**-UseTransaction**" always applies to the last one created, in fact, when a transaction is created after another, it is automatically (by default) nested inside it, so in situations like this, to complete latter created transactions, it is needed to complete the former as well.

```
PS HKCU:\> Start-Transaction          Create First Transaction

Suggestion [1,Transactions]: Once a transaction is started, only commands that get
hat transaction.
PS HKCU:\> New-Item X1 -UseTransaction      Create key X1 on First Transaction


   Hive: HKEY_CURRENT_USER


Name                           Property
----                           --------
X1


PS HKCU:\> Start-Transaction          Create Second Transaction

Suggestion [1,Transactions]: Once a transaction is started, only commands that get
hat transaction.
PS HKCU:\> New-Item X2 -UseTransaction      Create key X2 on Second Transaction


   Hive: HKEY_CURRENT_USER


Name                           Property
----                           --------
X2


PS HKCU:\> Complete-Transaction         Complete Second Transaction
PS HKCU:\> ls X*             List all keys that begin with X. None are returned
PS HKCU:\> Complete-Transaction         Complete First Transaction
PS HKCU:\> ls X*              List X* keys again, now both keys are returned
   Hive: HKEY_CURRENT_USER
Name                           Property
----                           --------
X1
X2
```

Figure 44: Example of two nested transactions and how they behave upon competition.

At the previous figure, there is the CMD step-by-step example of the behavior explained. If there were 5 transactions, all of them would need to be closed so the commands that use them would to be, in fact, committed.

9.7.   Independent Transaction

We can use independent transactions to overcome the limitations of the default "nested transactions" behavior. To create an independent transaction: "**Start-Transaction –Independent**".

```
PS HKCU:\> Start-Transaction    Start First Transaction

Suggestion [1,Transactions]: Once a transaction is started, only commands that get called
hat transaction.
PS HKCU:\> New-Item TR1 -UseTransaction    Create key TR1 on First Transaction


    Hive: HKEY_CURRENT_USER


Name                        Property
----                        --------
TR1


PS HKCU:\> Start-Transaction -Independent    Start Independent Second Transaction

Suggestion [1,Transactions]: Once a transaction is started, only commands that get called
hat transaction.
PS HKCU:\> New-Item TR2 -UseTransaction    Create key TR2 on Second Transaction


    Hive: HKEY_CURRENT_USER


Name                        Property
----                        --------
TR2
```

Figure 45: Example creating a default and independent transaction.

On the creation of the second transaction, it has no dependency with the first one, so it can be completed and the TR2 key will be created in the registry.

```
PS HKCU:\> Get-Transaction    Get Information on Current Transaction

RollbackPreference SubscriberCount Status
------------------ --------------- ------
             Error               1 Active


PS HKCU:\> Complete-Transaction  Complete The Second Transaction
PS HKCU:\> ls TR*           List all Keys that begin with TR, the Key TR2 was Created


   Hive: HKEY_CURRENT_USER


Name                        Property
----                        --------
TR2
```

Figure 46: Example creating a default and independent transaction.

The TR2 key was successfully created upon completion of the second transaction when the first was still active. Independent transactions do not count at the **"SubscriberCount"** when using the "Get-Transaction" for showing them, for this reason at Figure 46 this counter shows only 1 (and not 2).

9.8.   Conclusion of the Transaction

On native PowerShell, transactions can be used only for the registry operations, however, through the .NET integration we can use .NET types, classes and methods. The .NET framework has object types that allow using transactions, in this way, transactions can be much more powerful. At this moment, we are not going to expand on this subject yet because before that we need to build more advanced knowledge on variables and objects.

On the next figure, we give you a simple example of how a .NET type can be used inside PowerShell, in this case, when printing the variable, we notice that it becomes an object.

```
PS HKCU:\> [Microsoft.PowerShell.Commands.Management.TransactedString]$test = "hello"
PS HKCU:\> $test


Length
------
     5



PS HKCU:\>
```

Figure 47: Simple example for creating a string assignment that uses transactions.

10. Advanced Level: Dig Deeper into the PowerShell Variables

10.1. Introduction to the Environmental Variable Provider – Env:

The Windows operating system have some variables that store important information about both the logged-in user and the system itself. On the old CMD console that list of variables can be viewed just by typing: "**set**". You can execute CMD commands inside PowerShell using "**cmd /c**", so to list all system variables on PowerShell using the CMD command, just run: "**cmd /c set**".

As seen before with the Cmdlet "**Get-PSProvider**", PowerShell has a provider called "Environment" with a "drive" called "**Env**". Much like the Registry and Filesystem, we can "cd" into that drive and perform filesystem-like operations on it.

```
PS HKCU:\> cd Env:
PS Env:\> ls A*


Name                              Value

----                              -----

ALLUSERSPROFILE                   C:\ProgramData
APPDATA                           C:\Users\Abdelfattah\AppData\Roaming
```

Figure 48: Example of using the Env: provider.

At previous figure, we entered in the "**Env:**" drive and listed all system variables that starts with "**A**". To show all variables one just need to issue the "ls" without arguments. If you didn't "cd" into the Env: drive, you can still list variables using the "**env:**" prefix, so in the previous example "**ls env:A***" also works.

New environment variables can be created with the Cmdlet "New-Item", renamed with "Rename-Item" or deleted with "Remove-Item".

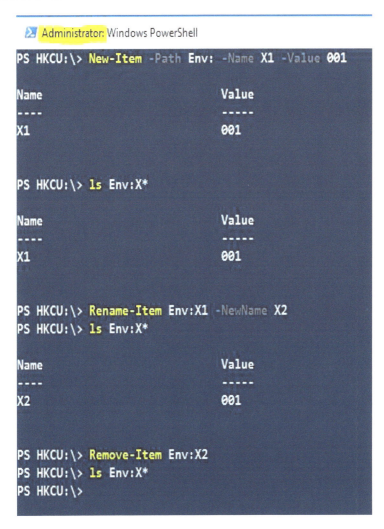

Figure 49: Filesystem-like operations with Env: provider.

More help information about "**Rename-Item**" (**ren** alias) or "**Remove-Item**" (**del**) can be obtained with: "**help ren**" and "**help del**".

10.2.   How to Read and Set Environmental Variables

If we "cd" inside the "Env:" drive, all previous examples would work without needing to explicitly refer the variables with the prefix "env:". The same applied when we explained about the registry provider and its operations.

```
PS HKCU:\> cd env:
PS Env:\> New-Item . -Name X1 -Value 002

Name                                    Value
----                                    -----
X1                                      002


PS Env:\> ls X*

Name                                    Value
----                                    -----
X1                                      002


PS Env:\> ren X1 -NewName X2
PS Env:\> cp X2 X3
PS Env:\> ls X*

Name                                    Value
----                                    -----
X3                                      002
X2                                      002


PS Env:\>
```

Figure 50: Working with Env without the prefix "env:"

At the previous figure, we did the same operations with Env but without explicitly using the "**env:**" prefix since we cd into it first. At this example, we used another alias called "**cp**" which is the Cmdlet "**Copy-Item**", this Cmdlet allows coping (in this case) one variable to another. To find out more about it, just type "**help cp**".

10.3. Setting Variables of Other PSDrives

We can access providers items as variables simply using the dollar sign before specifying the drive, for example: "**$env:x2**". This way of accessing as variable as the advantage of adding more ways of manipulating these data, for example, applying string operations on different provider items for changing or creating them.

Figure 51: Example of accessing provider items as variables for "Env" and "Alias".

Another advantage is being able to use the TAB key to autocomplete provider items, so you can simply type: "**$Env:**" +

<TAB_KEY> and the console will automatically be completed with the first item inside the "**Env:**" provider.

On the providers "Registry", "WSMan", "Function" and "Cert" we can't access as variables because they have more complex organization structure (for the 'Registry' we already saw that there's a hierarchy of keys and sub-keys are treated as properties).

To create a provider item, we just assign a value to the variable that represents it. All operations with this variable will affect the corresponding provider item.

```
PS C:\> $env:X3 = '88'        Creating the item X3 on Env Provider
PS C:\> $env:X3               Showing the X3 item of Env Provider as Variable
88
PS C:\> $env:X3 += $env:windir String operation on two different Env items - Concatenation
PS C:\> $env:X3
88C:\Windows
PS C:\> ls env:X3             Showing the same X3 item of Env Provider using Filesystem-Like Operation

Name                          Value
----                          -----
X3                            88C:\Windows


PS C:\> $env:X3 = ''          Deleting the X3 item, then Showing as Variable and as Filesystem-Like Operation
PS C:\> $env:X3
PS C:\> ls Env:X3
ls : Cannot find path 'X3' because it does not exist.
At line:1 char:1
+ ls Env:X3
+ ~~~~~~~~~
    + CategoryInfo          : ObjectNotFound: (X3:String) [Get-ChildItem], ItemNotFoundException
    + FullyQualifiedErrorId : PathNotFound,Microsoft.PowerShell.Commands.GetChildItemCommand
```

Figure 52: Example of operations with providers using its variable representation.

Note that after assigning the value '' to X3, automatically the item is removed, that can be verified when trying to access either as variable or as Filesystem-like operation. One practical application of the simple variable representation and its benefits is when there is a need to insert a new folder to the environment path variable.

For that we simply need to concatenate the desired folder to the end of the variable: "**$env:Path += 'C:\users'**".

10.4.   Environment.GetEnvironmentVariable Method

In addition to the two different ways of accessing and manipulating the environment variable (**env**), there is a third option using the .NET native integration with PowerShell. To get the value of a single environment variable:

[System.Environment]::GetEnvironmentVariable('<NAME >')

Where at the tag <name> it need to be replaced with the desired environment variable name. To list all available environment variables:

[System.Environment]::GetEnvironmentVariables()

The name inside brackets specify which .NET class it going to be used, the double colon is used to separate the class name from the method name. In the methods that have no arguments, they need to be written with trailing 'open and close' parenthesis. To either create a new environment variable or change a value of an existing one, the following command can be used:

[System.Environment]::SetEnvironmentVariable('<NAME> ' , '<VALUE>')

The **SetEnvironmentVariable** accepts two arguments for specifying which variable is to be created/changed and the respective value. The option for deleting an environment variable is similar to the way of using the variable access of a PSProvider seen earlier:]

[System.Environment]::SetEnvironmentVariable('<NAME>','')

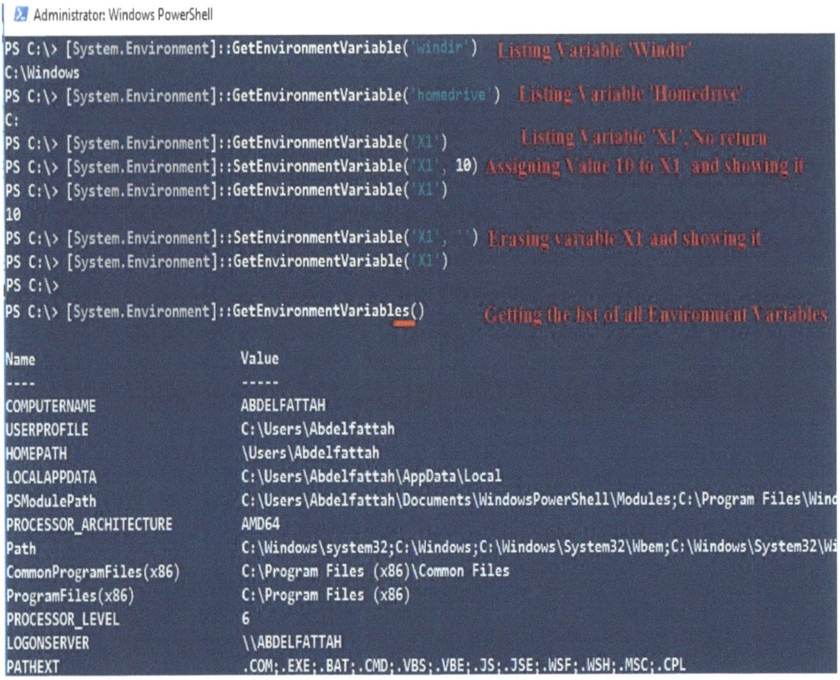

Figure 53: Example of environment variable manipulation with the .NET methods.

Note that when a variable that doesn't exist is listed, the console returns nothing at the line below. The last command's result for showing all environment variables was cropped.

10.5.   Introduction to PowerShell variable provider

From the providers list at Figure 51 it can be seen there is a provider called "Variable". This provider is responsible for controlling all PowerShell variables that are pertaining to the current PowerShell session. Just like the other providers, we can access and interact with this provider in two ways: variable representation and Filesystem-like operations. Since this provider controls all accessible variables, its variable representation can be replaced with the regular variable usage (only using the dollar sign "$").

For creating an item at this provider (variable), we can do it in three different ways:

- **$X2 = 100**

- **$variable:X2 = 100**

- **New-Item –Path variable: -Name X2 -Value 100**

To List the items:

- **$X2**

- **$variable:X2**

- **Ls variable:X2**

To remove an item (variable) there is only the Filesystem-like operation way because using the two other ways result at just assigning empty values to it: "**Remove-Item -Path variable:X3**". That command can, as well, be used with wildcards, in this way, to remove all items (variables) that start with "W": "**Remove-Item – Path variable:W***".

```
PS C:\> ls variable:c*        Listing Variables its names starts with C

Name                          Value
----                          -----
ConfirmPreference             High
ConsoleFileName
c                             20


PS C:\> $ConfirmPreference    Using $ to show the Value of Variable
High
PS C:\> New-Item -Path Variable: -Name C1 -Value 100   Creating a Variable in Filesystem-like operation

Name                          Value
----                          -----
C1                            100


PS C:\> Remove-Item -Path Variable:ConfirmPreference    Remove the Variable
PS C:\> ls variable:c*    Check the "C1" was Created and "ConfirmPreference" was Removed

Name                          Value
----                          -----
ConsoleFileName
c                             20
C1                            100


PS C:\> ls variable:    Show All items of the "Variable" Provider

Name                          Value
----                          -----
$                             variable:c*
?                             True
^                             ls
a                             5
args                          {}
```

Figure 54: Interacting with the "Variable" provider.

At the previous example, notice that we show the contents of the "ConfirmPreference" variable in two different ways. The last command's output for listing all variables was cropped.

10.6.   Using CmdLets of the PowerShell variable

The variable provider has also specific Cmdlets to interact with it. These Cmdlets allows us to accomplish the same results we

84

would in other ways (either with variable representation or Filesystem-like operations) and additional more complex operations not available at different methods. The examples shown here are of the first type (simple operations). In order to find out what CmdLets are available to interact with the Variable provider, as usual: "**Get-Command –Noun variable**".

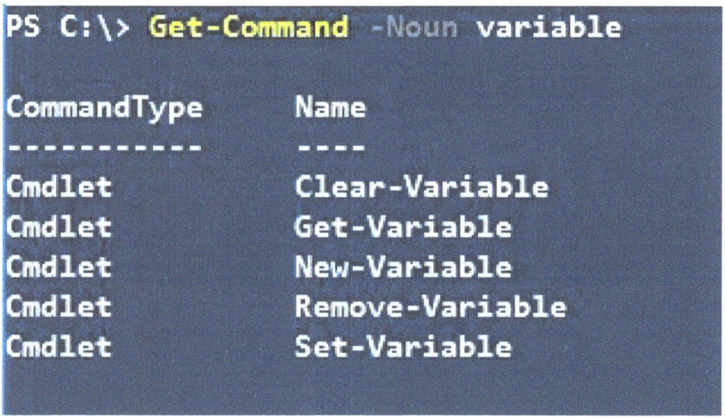

Figure 55: Listing Cmdlets that have "variable" as noun.

The CmdLets have intuitive names: "**Clear-Variable**" allows emptying the variable value, "**Get-Variable**" allows obtaining a variable's value, "**New-Variable**" allows creating a new variable, "**Remove-Variable**" allows removing a variable and "**Set-Variable**" allows changing/creating variables with corresponding values. You can issue the help documentation of each Cmdlet to find out more details (example: "**help New-Variable**").

```
PS C:\> New-Variable X10 -Value 000   Creating a new Variable X10
PS C:\> Get-Variable X10   Confirming it was created

Name                          Value
----                          -----
X10                           000


PS C:\> Get-Variable X10 -ValueOnly   List only its Value
000
PS C:\> Get-Content variable:X10     Another ways of listing only its Value
000
PS C:\> Set-Variable -Name X10 -Value 111   Changing the Value of X10
PS C:\> Get-Variable X10 -ValueOnly   Confirming the Change
111
PS C:\> Clear-Variable X10   Cleaning the Variable's Value
PS C:\> Get-Variable X10   Confirming the Change

Name                          Value
----                          -----
X10


PS C:\> Remove-Variable X10   Removing the Variable and then confirming it
PS C:\> Get-Variable X10
Get-Variable : Cannot find a variable with the name 'X10'.
At line:1 char:1
+ Get-Variable X10
+ ~~~~~~~~~~~~~~~~~
    + CategoryInfo          : ObjectNotFound: (X10:String) [Get-Variable], It
    + FullyQualifiedErrorId : VariableNotFound,Microsoft.PowerShell.Commands.
```

Figure 56: Simple specific CmdLets operations with the "Variable" provider.

One advanced usage of the specific variable Cmdlets is the possibility of creating read-only and constant variables.

```
PS C:\> New-Variable X1 -Value 000 -Description 'Readonly Variable' -Option ReadOnly
PS C:\> Remove-Variable X1
Remove-Variable : Cannot remove variable X1 because it is constant or read-only. If the variable is read-only, try the
specifying the Force option.
At line:1 char:1
+ Remove-Variable X1
+ ~~~~~~~~~~~~~~~~~~
    + CategoryInfo          : WriteError: (X1:String) [Remove-Variable], SessionStateUnauthorizedAccessException
    + FullyQualifiedErrorId : VariableNotRemovable,Microsoft.PowerShell.Commands.RemoveVariableCommand


PS C:\> Remove-Variable X1 -Force
PS C:\> Get-Variable X1
Get-Variable : Cannot find a variable with the name 'X1'.
```

Figure 57: Example of advanced usage of variable Cmdlet.

At the previous Figure is seen that the parameter "**-Option ReadOnly**" at the "**New-Variable**" Cmdlet allows creating a variable that cannot easily change its value or remove it. The only way to remove this variable is using the "**-Force**" parameter at the "**Remove-Variable**" Cmdlet. If the variable was created with "**-Option Constant**" there wouldn't be an option for removing it so it would exist until the console window is closed.

10.7.   Using the Dollar Sign with PowerShell Variable

The previously seen dollar sign '$' can be used to access and modify variable's values. When it is wanted to create a variable that has spaces on its name or special values, we can use the dollar sign associated with braces.

```
PS C:\> $hello = 44
PS C:\> ${hello World} = 555
PS C:\> ${hello World}
555
PS C:\> Get-Variable 'hello World'

Name                                    Value
----                                    -----
hello World                             555
```

Figure 58: Example of creating/changing files with variable notation.

When dealing with specific variable Cmdlet, the variable name that contains spaces can be specified enclosed in simple/double quotes.

That special notation can be used, also, to create and change files inside the Filesystem as shown in the next Figure:

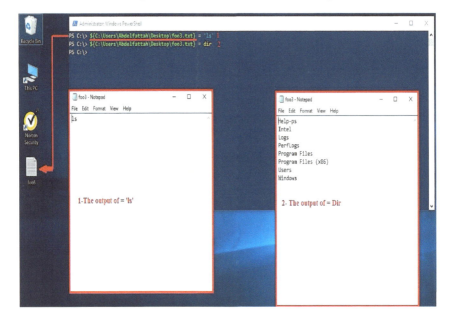

Figure 59: Example of creating/changing files with variable notation.

The braces were used to specify a file that didn't exist, upon setting a value to that "variable" the file was actually created. First it was created with its content being the text "ls", secondly it was created with its content being the information returned by the "dir" command. This task is not accomplished using the specific variable Cmdlets or any other method.

10.8.   Casting Values in PowerShell

PowerShell allows us to convert on-the-fly variable data between different types in a very simple manner. There is a way of converting variables to different types known as "Cast". The "cast" is the method of adding the desired type in a variable assignment before the value itself and enclosed with brackets. Let`s assume we want to convert a string in the Boolean type: **$n = [bool]"test"**. The "**$n**" variable will receive the value **TRUE** since at this conversion any value different than empty is considered "**TRUE**".

In another example, we might want to convert a string to the XML native PowerShell type:

$hello = '<a><d>0000</d></a>'

$hello = [xml]$hello

In the above example the "**$hello**" variable first received a string value and at the second line the type was converted to the "XML". Being XML the PowerShell interprets as an object. Being a XML object representation, the variable values can be accessed using dots. If we would like to everything inside the "**b**" tag:"**$hello.a.b**", it would return everything inside this tag (the tags "**c**" and "**d**" with their respective values). If we want to extract just the values of tags "**c**" or "**d**": "**$hello.a.b.c**" and "**$hello.a.b.d**"

```
PS C:\> $hello = "<a><b c='Hello'><d>0000</d></b></a>"   Variable receives string value
PS C:\> $hello                                            Printing the variable as string
<a><b c='Hello'><d>0000</d></b></a>
PS C:\> $hello = [xml]$hello                              Casting to XML type and printing
PS C:\> $hello

a                          Since the outermost TAG is the "a", it is the only one shown
-
a
b

PS C:\> $hello.a.b         Accessing everything inside tags a->b

c    d
-    -
Hello 0000

PS C:\> $hello.a.b.c       Accessing only the values of tags "c" and "d" inside "a->b"
Hello
PS C:\> $hello.a.b.d
0000
PS C:\>
```

Figure 60: Example of casting from String to XML type.

The casting method can be used to change different values as well: String->Integer, Integer->String, Float->Integer, etc. Note that the cast on the previous example was at the right side of the equal sign. This means that the value being assigned is casted before going to the variable and since the variable has not a specific defined type, it will accept anything. We can use the cast to change the variable type itself, in this way; the variable will have a static defined type that can only be changed latter with another explicit cast. To give an example, we can do: "**$a =[int] 5**" and latter "**$a = 'hello world'**". If we cast the variable itself instead: "**[int]$a = 5**" and after that: "**$a = 'hello world'**" it would give an error because the variable is explicitly casted of type string.

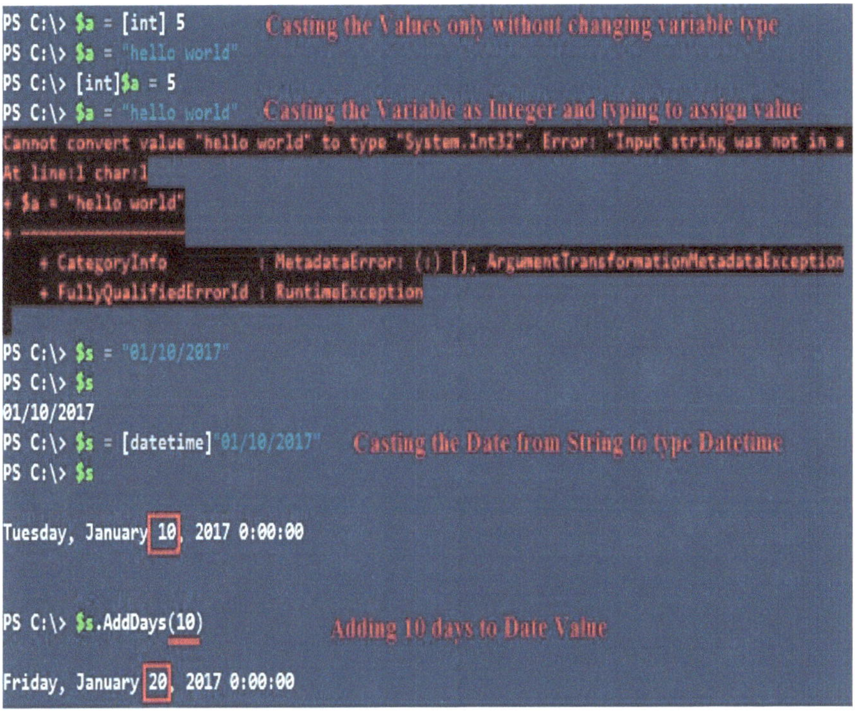

Figure 61: Other examples of casting variable itself and to DateTime.

On the previous figure, we can notice that once the variable **$a** was casted to integer, it would not accept to receive a string value. After that was shown an example of type datetime being casted from string and making a date operation with the variable.

10.9.   Introduction to Parameter Validation

Parameter validation is the concept of verifying whether a given string passes a pre-defined test designed to prevent input of incorrect data. One very simple example is a website registration form that does not allow you to register with an e-mail addresses that does not contain a "**@**".

Casts can be very useful for validating purposes as well. There are special kinds of functions that accept to be used inside a cast and allow creating validation rules at the time an assignment is made to a variable. To know more about all these functions, you can read this help: **"help about_functions_advanced_parameters"**.

Figure 62: Part of documentation on advanced function parameters.

As can be seen on the previous figure, the **"ValidateLength"** allows creating a validation rule in which verifies if the value assigned to a variable respects length restrictions. At the example given, it would only accept strings of length between **1** and **10**.

Another example is the **"ValidatePattern"** that allows inserting specific patterns that the string must comply at the assignment. If we want to create a variable that accepts only string values that begin with the letter **"h"**, we can do: **"[ValidatePattern('\Ah')]$test = 'hello'"**, in this argument **"\Ah"** specifies to the function to only allow strings that begin with the letter **"h"**.

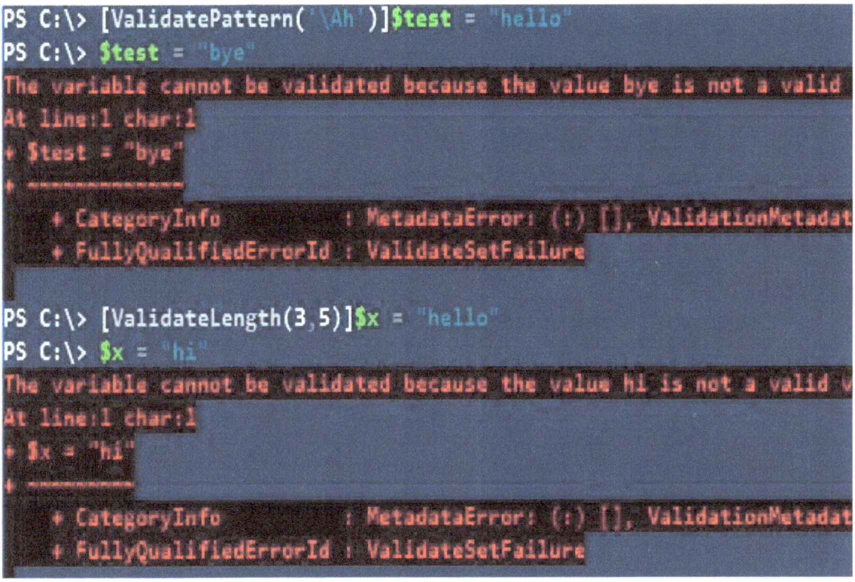

Figure 63: Example of using validations with cast.

At the examples, notice that once the variable is casted with the validation, it will only accept values that respect the rules defined. At the first line the assignment to "**hello**" worked because this string begins with "**h**". At the second line the assignment to "**bye**" resulted in an error because this string does not begin with "**h**". In the same way, using the "**ValidateLength**", it accepted "**hello**" because the length is between **3** and **5**, but didn't accept the string "**hi**" because it has length **2**.

10.10.   Easy Validating Parameter Input: Validateset and Validatescript

As previously mentioned, there are a number of other validation functions:

- **ValidateRange**: Verifies with a number is inside a specific value range;

93

- **ValidateScript**: One of most powerful ones, allows using operators and composing with them;

- **ValidadateNotNull**: Verifies if the value is not null;

- **ValidateNotNullOrEmpty**: Its name is self-explanatory;

- **ValidateSet**: Verifies if the value is one of the previous values expected.

To give an example of how to use the **ValidateSet**, let us suppose we want to verify if the string is either: "**dog**", "**cat**"or "**lion**":

[ValidateSet("dog","cat","lion")]$animal = "cat"

The "**ValidateScript**" allows using any kind of comparison (greater than: **-gt**, equal: **-eq**, less than: **-lt**, etc.) operator and logic ("**-and**", "**-or**", "**-not**", etc) operators combined to create complex rules. Let us imagine we want to verify if a value assigned is always greater than 5:

[ValidateScript({$_ -gt 4})]$number = 5

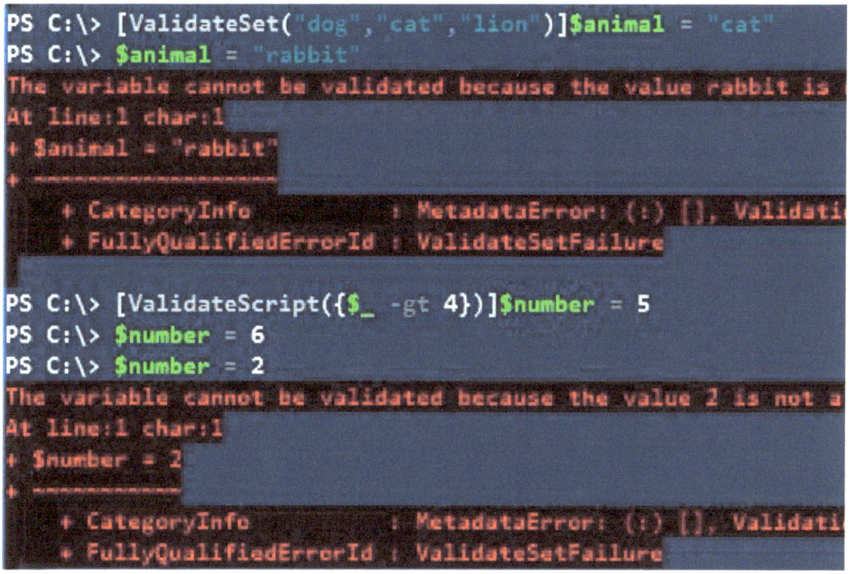

Figure 64: Example of using validations with cast: ValidateSet and ValidateScript.

Notice that when the variable "**$animal**" received the value "**rabbit**" it resulted in an error because this word is not in the validation list provided. To use the "**ValidateScript**" the verification must be enclosed in braces, the variable "$_" refers to the value being assigned. At the example, it verifies if the value is greater than (**-gt**) **4**. In the first and second assignments, it worked because the values were greater than **4** (5 and 6), the last one failed because it was lesser than **4** (2).

10.11. Parsing, Variable Expansion and Quoting

Now we are going to learn a little more about variables. We can join string values using the "**+**" operator, so if we want to print "hello world", we can create a variable to receive the value "world": **$var = "world"** and make the concatenation: **"hello " + $var**. We can accomplish the same goal using the "Syntactic Sugar". This is a special kind of syntax that allow creating strings using placeholders and assigning values externally, so it would rewrite as: **"hello {0}" –f $var**. If we would like to insert more variables, we just needed to use **$1**, **$2**, etc. This kind of syntax is used mainly when needing to interact with .NET functions and objects. The **"{0}"** is replaced with the **"$var"** value, that replacement is called "**variable expansion**"

Another way is using the implicit variable expansion, PowerShell does the expansion for you if the variable is inside a string that is defined in double quotes: **"hello $var"**. This works because the command is enclosed in double quotes, if single quotes are used the "**var**" is not expanded and is shown only as "**$var**".

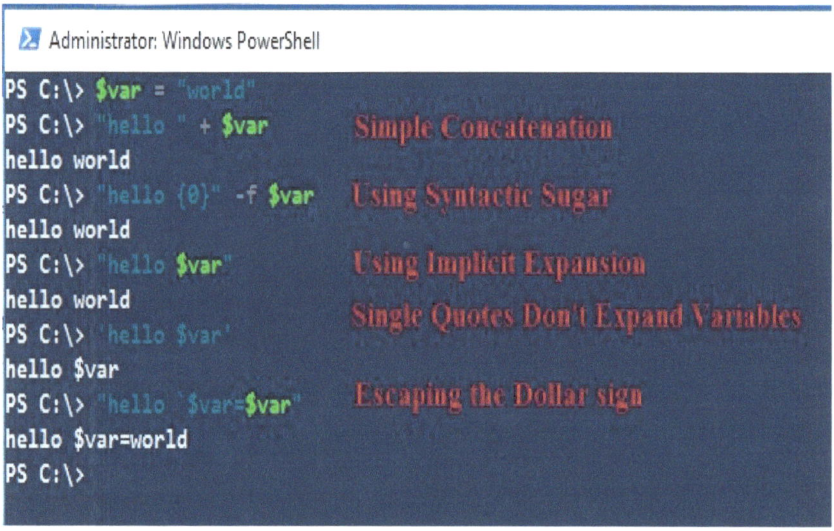

Figure 65: Different ways of doing the same task using variables.

It is possible to avoid the variable expansion when the variable is written inside double quotes, to accomplish this it is just needed to use the sign: `. This sign escapes the dollar sign, thus, avoiding the expansion. At the previous figure, the expansion was avoided to show the literal name of the variable with its respective value.

10.12.   Compulsory Arguments: Order to process components

As seen previously, the double quote allows the automatic variable expansion. It is important to stress out that some variables are objects, therefore, they have attributes that can be accessed using dots (.). In such cases, it is necessary to ask PowerShell to evaluate these variables first because, by default, it assumes that we want to print only the string representation of the object.

To exemplify this situation, imagine that we get the object that represents an OS service called "spooler": **$s = Get-Service spooler**. If we show the **$s** variable we'll notice that it is has different attributes: Name, Status and DisplayName. If we try to use the object inside a double-quote defined string, it will be expanded to its string representation, in other words, the object will be automatically casted to string at the variable expansion. In this case, it will print: **System.ServiceProcess.ServiceController**. So the commands: **[string]$s** and **"$s"** produce that same output.

If we wanted to print the process status inside the double quote, one would think that **"Spooler Status = $s.status"** would suffice, however,   it   produces: **"Spooler   Status =System.ServiceProcess.ServiceController.status"**.   The PowerShell evaluates the **$s** variable and treats the status as a regular string. To solve this issue we need to enclose the variable inside the "**$( )**", this makes the PowerShell evaluate first everything inside the "**$( )**" and then the rest of the expression: **"spooler = $($s.status)"**.

```
Administrator: Windows PowerShell

PS C:\> $s = Get-Service Spooler
PS C:\> $s                    Printing the full object

Status   Name                DisplayName
------   ----                -----------
Running  Spooler             Print Spooler


PS C:\> $s.Status             Printing only the object's status attribute
Running
PS C:\> [string]$s            Object string representation: Explicit cast
System.ServiceProcess.ServiceController
PS C:\> "$s"                  Object string representation: Implicit cast
System.ServiceProcess.ServiceController
PS C:\> "spooler = $s.status"  Trying to access the status attribute - Wrong way
spooler = System.ServiceProcess.ServiceController.status
PS C:\> "spooler = $($s.status)"  Correct way
spooler = Running
PS C:\> "My name is =$(Read-Host -Prompt "Enter Your Name")"  Example of Evaluation Precedence
Enter Your Name: Abdelfattah
My name is =Abdelfattah
PS C:\>
```

Figure 66: Examples of object variable expansion.

One other example that expressions enclosed in "$( )" are evaluated first is the final command at the previous figure. The data acquisition happens before the rest of the print operation.

10.13.   The PowerShell variable scope

Variable scope is very important when we are dealing with multiple variables to solve some complex problems. To illustrate this, open up the PowerShell ISE because now we will write some code that have more lines. Variable scopes can be defined using the following syntax:

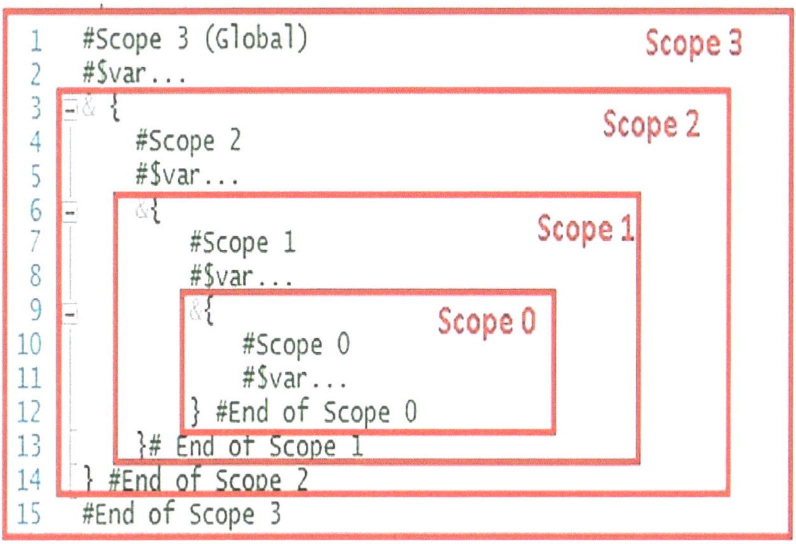

Figure 67: Example of scope definition

The variables defined inside each outer scopes are visible to the inner scopes, when variables have conflicting names, the value of the innermost scope is considered. That behavior can be changed when using the special declarations: **$global:<variable>** or **$local:<variable>**. In the former, the outermost variable scope is considered, in the latter, the innermost variable scope is applied.

```
1    #Scope 3 (Global)
2    $varA = 1
3    $varB = 10
4    □& {
5            #Scope 2
6            $varA = 2
7            $varB = 20
8    □      &{
9                #Scope 1
10               $private:varA = 3
11               $varB = 30
12   □           &{
13                   #Scope 0
14                   "VarA value: " + $varA
15                   "VarB value: " + $varB
16                   "VarA Global: " + $global:varA
17                   "VarA Local: " + $local:varA
18               } #End of Scope 0
19           }# End of Scope 1
20   } #End of Scope 2
21   #End of Scope 3
```

```
VarA value: 2
VarB value: 30
VarA Global: 1
VarA Local:
```

Figure 68: Example of variable scope assignment and usage

The **$varA** value was 2 because at the previous scope the assignment "**$private:varA = 3**" means that **$varA** variable assignment was, exclusively, valid inside that scope where it was performed. The **$varB** value is **30** because is the most recent value from an assignment, the **$global:varA** references the first and outermost **$varA** value (from scope 3). The **$local:varA** is nothing because the modifier "**$local**" forces it to look for the variables only defined inside that particular scope, since in the scope 0 no value was assigned to variable **$varA**, it returns nothing.

10.14. The PowerShell Scope Hierarchy

At any given scope, the variable's outermost scopes, values can be obtained using the "Get-Variable" Cmdlet. This Cmdlet counts the scope from 0 starting at the current scope to infinity number depending on the number of outermost scopes available. The syntax to get only the variable's value:

Get-Variable –Name <VAR> -Scope <N> -ValueOnly

Note from the next figure that at the innermost scope it is able to access all the outermost scopes. At the scope 0 the **$varA** was not rewritten/defined, for this reason, it was thrown an error when trying to access it and it returned nothing. It was possible to retrieve the value even from the private declaration from scope 1.

```
1   #Scope 3 (Global)
2     $varA = 1
3   =& {
4         #Scope 2
5         $varA = 2
6     =    &{
7             #Scope 1
8             $private:varA = 3
9     =        &{
10                #Scope 0
11                "VarA - 0: " + $(Get-Variable -name varA -Scope 0 -ValueOnly)
12                "VarA - 1: " + $(Get-Variable -name varA -Scope 1 -ValueOnly)
13                "VarA - 2: " + $(Get-Variable -name varA -Scope 2 -ValueOnly)
14                "VarA - 3: " + $(Get-Variable -name varA -Scope 3 -ValueOnly)
15            } #End of Scope 0
16        }# End of Scope 1
17    } #End of Scope 2
18    #End of Scope 3
```

```
Get-Variable : Cannot find a variable with the name 'varA'.
VarA - 0:
VarA - 1: 3
VarA - 2: 2
VarA - 3: 1
```

Figure 69: Example of accessing specific outermost scopes

Scopes can be created and obtained using directly the Commandline as well:

101

```
PS C:\> New-Variable -Name mytest -Value 5 -Option Private
PS C:\> $mytest
5
PS C:\> &{$mytest}
PS C:\>
```

Figure70: Example of accessing specific outermost scopes

The variable creation using the CmdLet has the same effect as: "**$private:mytest = 5**". Note that when creating a new scope, the value cannot be accessed since it was created as a private assignment.

11. Conclusion and Your First Mission

We discussed at previous that every time the PowerShell window is closed, all data pertaining that session is lost. We also saw that the profile creation could solve this; however, we did not teach how to do that. We leave this profile creation as an exercise for you, now you can use all the information and knowledge you learned from this book to find out and accomplish this goal.

Just to give some hint, you can start by finding out the help documentation about profiles issuing "**help profile**".

The Last Step

If you liked this Book please leave your review here **bit.ly/powershell5** , if not please send me your feedback to **Abdelfattahben@gmail.com**so I can update the eBook to make it more great for you and for other readers

Good Luck!

www.ingramcontent.com/pod-product-compliance
Lightning Source LLC
LaVergne TN
LVHW012316070326

832902LV00004BA/80